W9-BAP-461

Collective Bargaining In Education

Collective Bargaining In Education
A Casebook

AL H. NOTHEM
Saint Bonaventure University

ALLYN AND BACON
Boston   London   Toronto   Sydney   Tokyo   Singapore

Series Editor: Raymond Short
Series Editorial Assistant: Jo Ellen Caffrey
Production Coordinator: Marjorie Payne
Editorial-Production Service: Benchmark Productions
Cover Administrator: Linda Dickinson
Cover Designer: Suzanne Harbison
Manufacturing Buyer: Louise Richardson

Library of Congress Cataloging-in-Publication Data

Nothem, Al H.
    Collective bargaining in education: a casebook/Al H. Nothem.
        p. cm.
    ISBN 0-205-13322-3
    1. Collective bargaining--Teachers--United States--Case studies.
2. Collective bargaining--Government employees--United States--Case
studies.   I. Title.
LB2844.59.U6N68 1992
331.89' 0413711' 00973--dc20   91-24110
                                                                    CIP

Printed in the United States of America
10 9 8 7 6 5 4 3 2 1   97 96 95 94 93 92

For Ardythe

CONTENTS

Collective Bargaining
In Education

INTRODUCTION

This casebook was written with the following goals in mind:

(1) To help collective bargaining students, public administrators, and members of public policy boards understand central issues in and alternative solutions to some of the problems in public sector bargaining.

(2) To bring about a synthesis of theory and practice by acquainting readers with the practical aspects of collective bargaining that can be related to theory. The casebook provides opportunities to apply general concepts and knowledge to specific situations.

(3) To provide students and other readers with the opportunity to discover and develop their own methods of analyzing and dealing with problems. The case-discussion method of teaching encourages students to think for themselves. It also demonstrates that students can learn by working together.

(4) To provide a needed casebook dealing with collective bargaining in education.

The cases presented in this book illustrate important principles of bargaining and give readers a sense of the controversies and uncertainties unique to the public sector, especially education. Exposure to central issues and opportunities to develop alternative solutions to key problems are provided.

One of the requirements for certification as a school administrator, in most states, is knowledge of collective bargaining procedures and problem resolution in education. Typically, the candidate for certification as a chief school officer, principal, or business manager will fulfill this requirement by taking a graduate course in collective bargaining. Other school or municipal managers will meet this need through workshops, seminars, or other in-service courses. Some will suffer "baptism by fire" by learning all about negotiation at the table.

Given the demonstrated need for case material in public sector bargaining, this casebook will serve as a textbook for instructors using the case-discussion method and problem-solving format of instruction. It will also serve as a supplementary resource in other administration courses that touch on negotiation, and perhaps in related labor relations courses.

In addition, this casebook can be used as a reference handbook by public board members and administrators who have not had formal training in collective bargaining. Most public officials must negotiate with public employees, administer contracts, field grievances, and deal with ongoing negotiation problems. The casebook will provide insight for possible solutions.

The cases in this book are organized into four modules according to the salient issues of the case. Each module consists of five cases intended to engender a class discussion lasting approximately two hours. Three of the twenty cases deal with bargaining problems in public sector organizations other than education. City, township, and county governments have unique bargaining problems worth exploring. Analysis of these three cases illustrates the folly of having one state collective bargaining statute apply to all state public organizations and their employees.

The 20 cases in the book are based on real and imaginary situations. The characters and locations are the product of a combination of imagination and creativity. Often situations from a number of real cases are fused to create a disguised case.

After each case, appropriate questions are provided to guide the reader in case analysis.

The role of the discussion leader is to motivate participants to identify the major issues and problems, discuss them, and suggest alternative courses of action and solutions. In doing this, the participants must take a position on the issue and defend it. In addition, students will be expected to determine what generalizations can be made about the case. For example, how might one avoid this kind of situation in the future? The answer may call for the development of action plans as students put themselves in the places of leading characters.

The discussion questions that follow each case can be used to initiate case analysis. Discussion leaders and participants will usually supplement these with questions of their choosing.

The case-discussion method of instruction, widely used in legal and business education, is becoming increasingly popular in educational administration. Discussion method enthusiasts attribute the method's effectiveness to its focus on real problems rather than on just facts and theories. The writer has found that this method of teaching brings about a synthesis of theory and practice.

COLLECTIVE BARGAINING IN THE PUBLIC SECTOR: AN OVERVIEW

Collective bargaining in the public sector is truly a product of the sixties. It was one of the major events of the turbulent decade that historians claim shaped a generation. Although events during the forties and fifties kicked off waves of discontent and unrest by employees in the public sector, the tidal wave hit in the early sixties. Illegal strikes and job actions challenged the then-current laws prohibiting strikes.

In 1962, President John F. Kennedy issued Executive Order 10988 permitting federal employees to organize and bargain. Before that, in 1959, Wisconsin passed the first state law dealing with collective bargaining for state public employees. Public employees in other states noted this trend and began lobbying for bargaining laws. New York's Taylor Law mandating public sector bargaining became effective in September 1967. Several years later, Pennsylvania passed Act 195, which not only mandated collective bargaining but also allowed public employees to strike. State legislators could not withstand pressure by public employees who demanded the right to negotiate with their employers. Currently, all but a few states mandate or allow a form of collective bargaining for state public employees.

But not all public employees were clamoring for collective bargaining during the sixties. The largest group of public employees consisted of the teachers belonging to the National Education Association (NEA). In 1965, the NEA published a booklet entitled *Guidelines for Professional Negotiation*, which made a clear distinction between professional negotiation and collective bargaining. Appendix B of that document lists five major reasons why professional negotiation is better than collective bargaining. (National Education Association, 1965)

During the 1940s and 1950s most of the teachers in the United States belonged to a local teachers' association affiliated with a parent state education association and the NEA. The members considered these organizations to be professional associations, not unions, and at that time opposed any form of collective bargaining. *The Public Interest in How Teachers Organize*, a pamphlet published in 1964 by the Educational Policies Commission, warned, "It is not only harmful but fallacious to assume that the labor-management relationship applies to public schools. Teachers and Superintendents are not private employees, and school boards are not private employers. No owner or investor makes a profit, in the usual sense, from the employment of educators. In education all should be, and most are, engaged in pursuit of a common goal—the best possible education of students....Thus, the application of labor-relations practices is detrimental to the public welfare and to the professional and personal interests of teachers. It has even resulted in cases in which unionized teachers have refused to cross picket lines established around schools by unions in jurisdictional disputes with one another. This disregard for the welfare of children and the public is a flagrant rejection of the idea that education is a service profession." (Educational Policies Commission, 1964)

During the late sixties, the NEA lost dues-paying members to a competitor, the American Federation of Teachers (AFT), a teachers' union that successfully promoted collective bargaining by its members. The NEA decided to reconsider its position on labor relations as practiced by the AFT. Maybe those tactics were not as detrimental to the public welfare and to the professional interests of teachers as originally thought. By the end of that decade, the NEA was no longer distinguishing itself as a professional association. It was a union, and its members were bargaining collectively. Thus, within a somewhat short span of twenty-five years, the NEA changed from the self-proclaimed professional association to the largest militant teachers' union in the United States—strikes and all.

Governments and school districts as employers have special characteristics that affect and influence collective bargaining. Among these are:

(1) The absence of clear lines of distinction between management and rank and file, between employer and employee. Is the school building principal employer or employee? In some states, principals and teachers bargain as one unit. However, in most states principals are considered members of the management team and must be recognized as a separate unit in order to negotiate.

Sometimes consistency is of little consequence when public employer and public employees organize to form bargaining units. In one case, all the officers of the city fire department except the chief belonged to the fire fighters' union—in fact, the officers were the union negotiators for the unit. In the same city, police officers above a certain rank were not allowed to join the rank-and-file negotiating unit. They were required to negotiate as a separate unit.

(2) The more restrictive scope of bargaining in the public sector than in the private sector. Issues have often been limited and sometimes

prohibited by statutes and ordinances. Yet, the scope of bargaining broadens as employee empowerment grows. Employees demand to negotiate issues such as class size, curriculum, personnel evaluation procedure, agency fee, site-based management, teacher mentoring policy, the number of bus routes and runs, frequency of garbage pickup, the number of police in patrol cars, and the number of fire fighters on the fire trucks.

(3) The uncommonly large part of the government agency's budget that is made up of wages and salaries. This causes problems because negotiated salary increases significantly affect the budget and are extremely visible. One sure way to hold the line on taxes is to not give raises.

(4) The presence of the public as a "third force" that blurs identification of the employer. This has been especially true in education. The public demands a role in the negotiation process and often gets it. When citizens realize the impact collective bargaining has on education and on their public services, they demand more information and involvement. Having an opportunity to read about what the fact finder had to say is not enough. The public wants the opportunity to influence what is going on at the bargaining table.

(5) The question of whether all public employees should be covered by one collective bargaining statute. Or should state legislators enact separate bargaining laws for each of the various classifications of employees? Some states have established one bargaining law for "essential" public employees and another law for those who apparently are not so essential. Unless the strike factor is involved, the usual difference between these laws is the use of binding interest arbitration versus advisory fact finding as the final impasse procedure. Most states attempt to cover all public employees with one comprehensive collective bargaining law, for which amendments are commonplace.

The latest stage in the school reform phenomenon, ambiguously labeled restructuring, teacher empowerment, shared decision making, school-based management, or site-based management, among others, confuses and adds to the issues in education bargaining. Traditionally, labor unions have negotiated work agreements with the local school district's central administration. Both the unions and management have been organized to operate and negotiate at that level. If central administration agrees to share power with the district's individual schools, a host of new issues surface:

(1) Will central management really share decision making regarding important issues with individual schools? Critics of the "new" shared decision making concept claim that teachers have always been in on the decision making. Teachers deny that and contend that when they were consulted, the issues usually were insignificant and petty. Teachers expect site-based management to involve them in the major decisions.

(2) How will unions handle the diffusion of power when administrative decisions are shared with schools? The unions know how to deal

with central administration power. The union negotiated one contract for all employees represented by the bargaining unit. All employees were expected to deal with the administration through union representatives, whether they were dues-paying members or not. The administration provided contract interpretation guidelines which all middle managers were expected to follow in implementing the contract. The central clearinghouse concept would clearly begin to unravel if shared decision making decentralized contract administration.

(3) How can a union protect its members if each school sets its own policies and responsibilities? Under these conditions the structure and perhaps role of the union will surely change. Union flexibility to the point of decentralization of its power within the school district, as well as other options, will have to be considered.

(4) Will the teachers' new role in shared decision making deemphasize the importance of the union? With teachers sharing more meaningful managerial responsibilities, the importance of the union for those teachers is likely to change. As schools become more independent by opting for the new management programs, teachers will bond with the school's goals and activities. If the unions remain inflexible in opposing school-site programs, they stand to lose support and members.

(5) As parents, teachers, and even students take on added responsibility, what will be the role of the principal in site-based management? When the school is governed by a committee of parents, teachers, and others. the principal often takes on the role of a facilitator or ringmaster. A few schools have tried team management without a principal. The role of middle management changed as school districts experimented with leadership reforms that were claimed to improve the quality of education.

(6) At what point, if any, in site-based decision making do teachers jeopardize their employee status and their right to unionize as they perform more and more management activities? Experience with teacher empowerment reforms to date indicates that this may not become an issue. Many teachers who have been empowered through "restructuring" have found that they have neither the time nor the energy to make it work. School administrators have not been particularly willing to delegate important decisions to the rank and file. And the unions have not been inclined to support issues that could jeopardize their right to bargain collectively.

What is the future of public sector bargaining? Although no one seems to be predicting dramatic changes, responses to the questions posed so far make change inevitable. State statutes will be amended and fine-tuned. The consensus seems to be that public sector collective bargaining, as we know it, will change but will not go away.

PART ONE

WHO WILL NEGOTIATE?

Collective bargaining should not be left to amateurs.

When private sector industry conducts collective bargaining, both labor and management are represented by skilled and experienced negotiators. Yet, research and experience show that public sector employer and employee groups were ill prepared to deal with the conditions confronting them when states mandated that public employers and public employees bargain in good faith. Without enough experienced negotiators to go around, many small municipalities and school districts were forced to go "in-house." Crash programs provided limited training for those who would be sitting at the table. But these programs proved inadequate. Thus, "do-it-yourself" bargaining often resulted in embarrassing situations and sometimes shattered images for both employers and employees.

In one case, a seven-member school board selected three of its own members to negotiate for the district. The teachers and three board members negotiated a contract that was then rejected by the board by a 7-0 vote. In another instance, the negotiators in a small township failed to put oral agreements into writing as they were made. Many weeks later they could not remember exactly what had been agreed to, so they started all over.

During the early years of public sector bargaining, novice teacher negotiators found themselves confronted with a favorite school board proposal—that teachers adopt a more professional attitude and responsibility. The public expressed concern. If all was going well in the school, why were boards demanding contract language that called for "teachers who are prompt, keep appointments with parents, maintain discipline, and report infractions of rules or standards"? The teachers were doing that anyway, weren't they? And if things were as they should be at the school, why were teachers demanding language that guaranteed that "teachers will not be required to teach outside their competencies"? Were school boards and administrators forcing teachers to teach subjects and grades for which they were not prepared and certified? The public had reason to be concerned.

Many problems could have been avoided if the parties had been given time to prepare for bargaining and the responsibilities of their roles. Yet, because of premature and ill-defined mandated collective bargaining laws, both employee and employer groups in the public sector discovered that they were poorly prepared to deal effectively with negotiation. They learned that preparation for effective negotiation takes time—more time than the average employer or employee can afford. The employees looked to professional union negotiators to represent them at the table. Employers hired professional negotiators wherever they could find them.

SELECTING THE EMPLOYEE REPRESENTATIVE

Who should negotiate on behalf of the employees? In most states, the labor relations agency, such as a public employment relations board, has a hand in helping employees select their negotiation representative. Many consider this to be one of the most important functions of the agency. The selection process is most often an election by secret ballot. Through a representative election, the employees choose the organization to represent them in collective bargaining. Ordinarily, the representative who receives a simple majority of the votes cast is the winner. In rare and exceptional circumstances, the winner must have received the votes of a majority of the members in the unit. If a majority of the employees vote against affiliation with an organization, the local association decides who among its members will represent it at the bargaining table.

Most public sector bargaining laws require exclusive representation—that is, the organization that receives the majority of the employees' votes cast during an election becomes the exclusive bargaining agent for all employees in the bargaining unit. All workers are required to accept the representation services of the winning organization whether they want to or not. Employees who voted for the other representative or for neither organization may be unhappy with the outcome, but they must accept it. An example illustrates this problem.

A school bargaining unit of 100 teachers holds an election to decide its bargaining representative. About one-third of the teachers favors one teachers' union, another one-third favors another bargaining representative, and approximately one-third opposes any union representation. Seventy teachers vote in the representative election. If only thirty-seven, or about 52 percent of those voting, opt to be represented by

XYZ Union, that union will then represent all 100 teachers, although only a few more than one-third of all the teachers voted for that union. A minority of employees control the union and determine the issues to be negotiated, approve or disapprove the contract, and decide whether to strike.

Statutes and policies that authorize such methods of determining bargaining representation have been criticized by both management and labor. Other critics have called into question the inequities of exclusive representation. Exclusive representation prohibits employees who object to unionization from personally negotiating with the employer. Courts usually have upheld decisions that denied nonunion members a vote on contract decisions made by the union. Nonunion members have not been happy with these decisions. They want the right to wield more influence on contract decisions that affect their lives.

The support for exclusive representation is based on the need for union security. The supporters of exclusivity claim that it balances the power and advantages of the employer. In addition, exclusive representation helps to define and stabilize the labor force and avoid splintering of negotiation strength. When the union successfully negotiates agency shop or agency fee, it has a means of disciplining "free riders" in the work force. In most public jurisdictions, an agency shop or agency fee provision in the collective bargaining agreement requires nonunion employees in the bargaining unit to pay a prorated fee to the union. This so-called fair-share payment usually excludes the union costs of its political activities. Unions contend that because they must represent all employees in the bargaining unit under exclusive representation, all employees reap the benefits of that bargaining process and should share its cost. A question often asked is: Does an exclusive union really reduce confusion and rivalry among the workers, as it is intended to do?

More than one-third of the states prohibit agency fee or agency shop clauses in bargaining contracts. These states have passed right-to-work laws. These statutes prohibit an employer or union from requiring a worker to join or pay dues to an exclusive bargaining agent or to any other union in order to work. Unions vehemently oppose this law because it eliminates an effective form of union security. States with right-to-work laws are known as the right-to-work states.

A most important aspect of public sector bargaining is the way employees are grouped into bargaining units. Most states attempt to avoid fragmentation. Some states, such as Wisconsin, limit the number of bargaining units to a set number of occupations. Again, the public sector borrowed from the private sector by adopting much of its criteria for determining appropriate bargaining units.

Among the factors in determining the make up of a unit are:

(1) Community of interest. Employees sharing the same goals and interests and having comparable salaries, benefits, duties, and working conditions may form an appropriate unit.
(2) Desires of employees. Employees' desires may be taken into consideration in an informal consultation or in a formal procedure such as an election of the representative unit.
(3) Geographic proximity and location of the employees. Opportunities to communicate and interact are an important factor for an appropriate unit.
(4) State statutory considerations, if applicable.
(5) Prior history of bargaining in the organization, if one exists.

The question of who is eligible to belong to specific public sector bargaining units and how they are organized is still an issue. Policy and practice vary from state to state and often within state borders. Some states allow middle-management personnel to belong to the same unit as rank-and-file subordinates. In other states, school support personnel, such as librarians, nurses, and guidance counselors, are eligible to join the teachers' unit. At least one state allows permanently certified teacher substitutes to belong to the professional teachers' union. One small city in New York State negotiates with a fire fighters' union comprising all fire fighters, including all officers, except the fire chief. In fact, the lieutenants and captains usually represent the union at the bargaining table. The fire fighters claimed that all personnel except the chief share a common community of interest and must work closely together. The same city negotiates with two police bargaining units; one includes all gold-braid officers above a certain rank, and the other unit is made up of patrol officers.

Significant to the organization of and eligibility for membership in bargaining units is the way *community of interest* is defined and represented. If the definition of *community* is broad and flexible, almost any group of employees can claim interest in forming a bargaining unit. The usual result is fragmentation as employees scramble to form units based on special interests. In one New York case, management, wishing to accommodate employees, recognized two separate bargaining units, each made up of employees representing different communities of interest. Secretaries, custodians, bus drivers, and other employee groups were represented in both negotiating units. Decisions like these are the root of the bargaining problems reflected in Case 1, "Divide and Conquer."

Organizations fragmentize when membership in a department is accepted as a community of interest for bargaining purposes, as is the case in many county government organizations. Bargaining is conducted at the department level, with department administrators in charge. Each department adopts its own set of personnel policies. In the decentralized world of county government, deprived of strong, unifying, central authority and a uniform county personnel policy, administrative control is fragmented, with each department left to fend for itself. This weak management structure influences the form and substance of bargaining in county organizations and is addressed in some detail in Part Three, Case 13, "But What About...?"

MANAGEMENT'S BARGAINING REPRESENTATIVE

The composition of and ratio of the membership of management's negotiation team remains an unresolved issue. Discussions of the issue include, at least, the following questions:

(1) Should board members serve on the negotiating team?
(2) Should a board member ever be the chief negotiator?
(3) Should the board's chief executive officer serve on the negotiating team?
(4) Should the board's chief executive officer ever serve as the chief negotiator?
(5) Should middle managers be members of management's negotiation team?
(6) Should middle managers at least be represented on the negotiation team?
(7) Should a middle manager ever serve as the chief negotiator?
(8) Should management hire a negotiator?
(9) How many people should be on management's negotiation team?

Authorities do not agree on an ideal size and makeup of management's negotiation team. A larger team has the advantage of broader representation, so that more constituencies are aware of what is being discussed at the table. Broader representation also provides opportunities for appropriate personnel to be present and thus influence decisions on critical issues. A smaller negotiating team has the advantage of less formality and perhaps fewer and shorter caucuses. With smaller numbers, the members of the negotiating team can get to know the viewpoints of other members on all issues more readily, thereby facilitating decision making. The advantages of one size team often are the disadvantages of the other.

Who should negotiate for management? What is the role of the elected policy maker—the member of the board? Most advisors, including those in state and national organizations, discourage board members from serving as the chief negotiator for management. Among the reasons cited are:

(1) Board members have not had the competency nor the knowledge that negotiation requires, nor have they had the time to prepare adequately.

(2) Boards have been placed at a strategic disadvantage when members negotiated. Board members have found it difficult to oppose ratification of an agreement they personally negotiated. Incredibly, though, sometimes they did just that. Case 2, "Three Out of Five Is Not a Majority," addresses the problems that can surface when board members negotiate. Obviously, not all small boards have the advantage of knowing the viewpoints of members.

(3) Board members frequently have lacked detailed information about the organization and personnel necessary to carry on successful negotiations.

Nevertheless, a number of small public systems have successfully used the president or another member of the board as the chief negotiator. Many resource experts agree that a small minority of board members—perhaps one or two—serving in low profile on the negotiating team has advantages.

Whether any board members sit on management's negotiating team or not, the board, council, or legislature has a critical role. A primary responsibility of that role is to appoint and approve the members of management's negotiating team and the team's chief negotiator. The policy-making body also must set the negotiation guidelines and parameters for the management team. In this regard, the board serves as ongoing advisor to the negotiating team. And, finally, the board must ratify the final agreement.

The chief executive officer of a public organization has a crucial role in the negotiation process. This person occupies a pivotal position in the preparation for and conduct of negotiations. The board's chief executive officer frequently represents management at the table and speaks for the organization. In that capacity, this person also represents and speaks for the public. In a few states, such as New York and Connecticut, the superintendent of schools is responsible for contract negotiations and signs the approved contract for management. As advisor to the board, the chief executive officer generates issues for the organization's package of bargaining proposals. When tempers flare, this person is expected to mediate and, when negotiation bogs down, to come up with alternative proposals. The chief executive officer also supplies required basic information to both parties so that negotiation proposals are based on comparable data.

With the contract signed, the chief executive officer plans the administration of the agreement. Failure to follow through with this administrative procedure puts the organization in jeopardy of a host of grievances. Contract administration is the process of interpreting and implementing the collective-bargained agreement. A single interpretation of the contract by the management team is crucial when more than one administrator must implement the contract provisions. Building principals should not have to guess how new contract language is to be interpreted. Failure to administer the contract adequately causes some of the problems involved in Case 4, "The Principal's Revolving Door," and in Case 17, "Drifting into the Strike Zone."

Some authorities believe that the chief executive officer should not be on the negotiating team. They feel that the superintendent can be more effective as an advisor to both negotiation teams by remaining on the sidelines. If the school district does not hire a professional negotiator, the chief executive officer is most likely to be designated negotiator for the organization. In a large public organization, the role of negotiator often is delegated to an assistant or associate administrator. Case 3, "The Naive Town Supervisor," suggests what can happen when an inexperienced, incompetent chief executive officer in the form of a town official takes over negotiation.

MIDDLE MANAGEMENT'S MUDDLE

The most battle-scarred to emerge from the early rounds of negotiations were the administrators classified as middle management. High on any list of hard-and-fast bargaining rules appears the adage "Never say never." An exception to that rule may be found in another: "Middle managers never serve as chief negotiator for the organization." Building principals who negotiate are a good example. When principals negotiated, they jeopardized their professional obligations. Haggling with teacher negotiators by night blemished the principal's image as an instructional leader and supervisor by day. The two roles proved incompatible.

The smaller the school district, the more important is the professional relationship between the principal and the teacher. Unfortunately, it was in the smaller school districts and other public organizations that middle managers were pressed into service bargaining for management. When the chief executive officer, for whatever reason, did not serve as chief negotiator for management, the middle manager was drafted. Frequently, the middle manager was the only other administrator in the organization.

On the other hand, when middle managers were excluded from negotiations altogether, another kind of problem emerged: the need for an opportunity for middle managers to provide input when it was needed. Middle managers must be involved, at least, as consultants and advisors in contract negotiations with employees they supervise. They deserve the opportunity to review negotiation issues and then suggest revisions of those issues. The middle manager must administer the negotiated contract at the department or building level. It is the middle manager who will implement the contract conditions, field the questions regarding interpretation, and suffer the first shot in the grievance procedure. The middle manager must have a full understanding of contract terms in order to not unknowingly violate that contract.

In some cases, the negotiation process has eroded the middle manager's authority to exercise managerial prerogatives. In education, for example, the teacher empowerment movement has, on occasion, ignored or circumvented the traditional role of the principal. Advocates of shared decision making theorize that the practice allows middle managers more time to deal with the really important decisions and tasks. They argue that teacher empowerment gained through collective bargaining need not diminish the leadership role of the principal. Advocates of teacher empowerment claim that constructive bargaining can lead to a stronger partnership between employer and employees. Case 4, "The Principal's Revolving Door," mirrors these problems.

Opinions differ concerning whether administrators and supervisors should organize to bargain collectively in their own behalf with the board. The 1980s saw a dramatic increase in the number of middle-manager bargaining units. Authorities predict that the number of administrators forming bargaining units will continue to increase.

Before the spectacular growth of public sector bargaining in the sixties, middle management supervisors commonly belonged to the same organizations or associations as the employees they supervised. At one time in education, all professional employees, including the superintendent, principals, support staff, and teachers, were eligible for membership in some of the same local, state, and national professional organizations. Frequently, school administrators held state and national offices in organizations such as the NEA. Collective bargaining changed that when it assigned middle management to an adversarial position. Administrators and supervisors were no longer welcome in the employees' organization. Middle management found that it was lonely and cold out there alone. In their haste to appease and settle with employee unions, legislative boards and their chief executive officers passed over middle management personnel, failing to notice their frustration and distress. When middle management organized and demanded recognition to bargain collectively, the superintendent and school board expressed dismay. Why was the administrative team falling apart? At that point, it was impossible to convince middle managers that they really had been a part of an administrative team all along. They knew better.

Collective bargaining by middle management is not allowed in all states. Where it is legal, opinions differ concerning whether it is appropriate and how well it is working. Those who oppose bargaining by administrators question whether supervisors can function as supervisors and managers if they belong to a union. Will they perform as loyal and efficient members of the management team? As a member of a bargaining unit, will the individual manager feel free to make appropriate administrative decisions without consideration for the union viewpoint? Experience to date demonstrates that middle managers who consider themselves an integral part of a management team are much less inclined to seek bargaining rights. Case 5, "The Meddling Middle Managers," deals with this problem.

Should the school district appoint an outside negotiator—a "hired gun"—to negotiate for management? Although the employment of a professional negotiator has, as one might expect, advantages and disadvantages, most authorities on the subject say yes. A major disadvantage is that the professional negotiator does not have to live with the negotiated contract. Another disadvantage is that the negotiator may not be available for meetings when the local teams are ready. Then, too, informal, ongoing interaction and communication between the negotiating parties might be hampered because the negotiators are just not around.

A major advantage of using a hired negotiator is the experience this person brings to the procedure. Chances are the professional negotiator will also be up-to-date on recent developments and bargaining laws. The negotiator can serve as a buffer between the union and management when serious problems crop up at the bargaining table. The professional negotiator is likely to suggest options for settlement that neither party has considered. When local personality clashes develop, the professional knows how to cool things down and get the proceedings back on track.

THE PUBLIC AND NEGOTIATIONS

The public is concerned about and confused by what has been going on in public sector bargaining. The public is confused by and upset about the "them-and-us" attitude perceived to exist between management and employees. Studies and experience demonstrate that the bargaining process, including grievance procedures, changed the relationship between employers and employees in the public sector. The public has sensed a deterioration of morale on the part of school board and other public legislators. An increasing number of board members of public bodies have resigned after short terms in office.

Current collective bargaining procedures often prohibit the public from knowing what has gone on during the bargaining process until the contract is signed and decisions are irreversible. By the time new salary agreements and revised policies are known, it is too late to do anything about them. Citizens charge that this situation represents a loss of their right to control the levels of public spending and taxation. In some communities, indeed in some states, the public has demanded a public airing of all proposals to be negotiated. If public officials and unions want to avoid the prospect of a third party—the public—at the negotiating table, they must see to it that citizens are informed of the issues being negotiated and of the progress of negotiations. Community citizens need to be reassured that all is going well and that they have not lost touch with their elected officials.

RESTRUCTURING'S EFFECT ON
WHO WILL NEGOTIATE

Restructuring—the current buzzword in educational reform—has the potential to dramatically change educational collective bargaining as we know it. The extent of its impact on bargaining depends on which of the many "forms" of restructuring is implemented. Shared decision making, teacher empowerment, school-based management, and site-based management, among others, have all been labeled forms of restructuring. Yet, when put in place, none of the above really "restructure" schools. At best they adjust the power base or assign new roles to school and community personnel. An exception to this is the suggestion made by a Carnegie Forum on Education report, *A Nation Prepared: Teachers for the 21st Century*, that schools should be run by a committee of teachers instead of by principals. That entails restructuring. However, significant changes have been made within the same old school structures.

The term *restructuring* appeared in the literature during the late 1980s, in reports by the National Governors' Association and the Education Commission of the States. These and other reports generally called for a redistribution of power within the schools, rather than a restructuring. It was thought that a redistribution of power would lead to more effective decision making and, in turn, to more effective schools. Some decisions regarding time allocations, budget, staffing, materials, and so forth would be delegated to the local school by the central office. At the school level, teachers, parents, community representatives, and sometimes students would share in the new-found decisions. Thus, those most closely affected by decisions would have a role in making those decisions. The teachers would feel "empowered" in that they would have more influence over and control of professional issues. The principals would feel "empowered" in that they could influence and control budgetary and staffing issues, among others. It was not intended that shared decision making develop into a tug-of-war between any two or more education factions, as it has in some cases. Collaboration was proposed as a means of improving the quality of instruction in particular and of education in general—a form of reform.

Both of the major teachers' organizations—the NEA and the AFT—have lent support to the concept of teacher empowerment, with some reservations. If this brand of "reform" succeeds, how will the unions deal with the many autonomous schools as the personnel therein attempt to control their destiny? Will the teachers' new role in shared decision making deemphasize the importance of the union? If so, who will negotiate for the union? What will happen when a union teacher files a grievance because a body of peers ruled that teacher incompetent? How will the union deal with that? What will happen when teachers volunteer for extra duties but the contract calls for extra pay for these duties? Will the contract agreement negotiated by the union's central negotiating team and the district's central administration hold true? How will unions handle the diffusion of power when administrative power is shared with the schools? How can unions protect their members if each school sets its own policies and responsibilities? Who will negotiate for the teachers?

Will central management really share decision making regarding important issues with individual schools? Will the principal in the local school be required to share heretofore administrative decisions with the building union representative? As individual schools become more autonomous, how will personnel identify with the labor contract negotiated by central administration? Will central administration continue to negotiate the "district" agreement with the unions? Who will negotiate for management?

These and many other questions must be addressed as "restructuring" becomes a reality.

CASE ONE

DIVIDE AND CONQUER

Craig Logan, president of the Humbolt Nonteaching Association, tapped on the boardroom door and, without waiting for a response, flat-out entered to take his place at the table in the center of the room. He was obviously upset. Mark Haverquist, State Association representative and negotiator, along with several members of the local employee negotiating committee, trailed in after Craig and promptly found their places beside him. Seated across the table were the members of the Humbolt School District negotiating team: Don Garvin, hired negotiator; Wayne Frank, new district superintendent; and Betty Weiler, school board member.

Craig Logan broke the silence, "We find the district's proposals for revision of our contract unreasonable and prejudicial, to say the least. They are unacceptable." Struggling to control emotion and anger, Craig continued,

"Frankly, we wonder where they came from. Clearly your proposals do not reflect the settlement you made with employees in the Support Staff Group. We have some knowledge of that negotiation and settlement. The proposals you gave us tonight were never presented to the Support Staff Group."

"That is correct," Don Garvin interrupted. "We are not negotiating the support staff contract. Again I must remind you those employees settled with a three-year agreement.

When the board granted your petition for recognition as a separate negotiating unit so that you could affiliate with your state and national organizations, you gave up the Support Staff Group. You turned on your fellow workers who wanted to maintain amicable in-house negotiations.

You got greedy. You wanted an outsider to negotiate for you, and that's what you have."

"That's enough!" shouted Mark Haverquist while pounding the table. "Everyone in this room knows why these courageous workers bucked the system and joined our state organization. They got tired of just taking what the district offered every year. They were falling farther and farther behind comparable workers in other school districts in wages and benefits. The board should not have approved both negotiating units. Custodians, mechanics, and bus drivers are included in each unit. The only nonteaching employees who had the good sense to join our association as a group are the cafeteria workers. This division has caused real morale problems in the district. I also want to remind you, Garvin, that you owe your job negotiating for this district to this unit. I suggest we stop the bull and get on with negotiations."

Garvin smiled. "That's what I'm here for. Since we have exchanged proposals, I suggest we caucus. Maybe your association can get its act together and give us a counterproposal yet this evening."

"We are not even going to try," said Haverquist through clenched teeth. "We intend to discuss your outrageous proposals with our members before we respond. It is difficult for us to believe that the district board came up with these provocative suggestions. We can set a date for another meeting, if you wish. I hope by that time you will have regained your sanity."

BACKGROUND: THE HUMBOLT DECISION

Why would a school board allow a relatively small number of nonteaching employees to divide into two negotiating units, one of which became affiliated with state and national organizations? That is a question local administrators and school board members asked each other when they heard about the controversial "Humbolt decision" two years ago.

Wayne Frank applied for the superintendent position in Humbolt when he heard that the board was accepting applications. Jim Burak, superintendent at Humbolt more than thirty years, had decided to retire. Wayne considered the Humbolt superintendency a step up from his current position as superintendent of the Owens Central School, a much smaller district about fifty miles north.

The opportunity to bring up the Humbolt decision presented itself during one of the interview sessions Wayne had with Superintendent Burak. They were discussing how the process of collective bargaining had changed the role and operations of the superintendent.

Jim Burak was reminiscing, "I'm going to miss much of this when I leave. Many teachers here have been with me for over twenty years; some of them were here when I came thirty-three years ago. I'm proud to say most of them are my close friends. The one thing I'll not miss is the damn negotiations. That almost cost me some of those friends."

Wayne Frank said, "I'm glad you brought up the subject of negotiations. There is one thing I've been meaning to ask you. Why has the Humbolt district agreed to negotiate with two separate support staff units? Each has a few of the same kinds of employees, like custodians."

"Because I wanted it that way, that's why!" growled Burak. "No, that's not exactly the way it was," he corrected apologetically. "One day a few members of the Support Staff Group told me that they wanted to call a vote for affiliation with the state and national organizations. When I asked why, they just said that it was becoming more and more difficult to get an employee to do the negotiating. The employee negotiator was getting a lot of pressure from the membership to press for higher salaries and more benefits. This, he felt, was difficult to do under the circumstances. Some of their members felt that negotiations should be conducted on a more impersonal level by a professional negotiator. And they could get one if they joined the state organization."

"I had the same situation in the Owens district after the first couple of contracts," said Wayne, "and eventually they joined the parent union."

"That's what we thought was happening here," responded Burak. "Then, several days after that first visit by a representative of cafeteria employees, a group of secretaries asked to see me after school. Cindy Robbins, a secretary who spoke for the group, said they were opposed to unionization, as were other members of the group. They objected to paying state and national dues and they saw no need for a professional negotiator. A vote to affiliate would probably pass by one or two votes, they estimated. It was this group who suggested two organizations—one for those who wanted to affiliate and one for those who wanted no change."

"Didn't the board object to dealing with two negotiating units?" asked Wayne.

"No, not really. Since I was district negotiator, they left it up to me," answered Jim.

Wayne said, "When interviewed by your board president, I admitted I felt uneasy about the two nonteaching negotiating units. I suggested the district hire a negotiator for all contracts. I don't feel all that qualified."

"Hell, I didn't either. My first confrontation with a union negotiator, Mark Haverquist, ended with both of us filing an improper practice charge. In time we both backed off and decided to try getting along. The good news for you is that the employees are talking about getting back together in one association. They don't see that Mark has gained that much in the two contracts he negotiated. Cindy's support staff members are in the middle of a two-year contract, with one year to go."

"Whatever the outcome of that, I still want a hired negotiator to handle bargaining. I think I will have plenty to do trying to fill your shoes in other ways," said Wayne.

"Before bargaining, there was a strong sense of family in this district. In defiance of the negotiation process, some of that feeling remains. I hope the district's 'hired gun' doesn't blast it all away," finished Jim.

PRELUDE: A HOPE SHATTERED

Dr. Wayne Frank received a three-year contract as the new superintendent of the Humbolt Central School District. Jim Burak wished him luck and moved to Myrtle Beach, where he and his wife purchased a five-room retirement condominium on the beach.

The board hired Don Garvin, a professional negotiator and professor at the local county campus of the State University System, as district negotiator. Professor Garvin, with several years of negotiating experience, had established a negotiation service office in the area.

Mark Haverquist persuaded the members of the State Association to hold off on the merger vote decision until after negotiations for the next contract. He reminded his group that its contract was the first to be renegotiated under the new administration and that the district would be represented by a tough, professional negotiator.

Dr. Frank scheduled a planning meeting of the district negotiation committee, which now included Don Garvin, district negotiator, and Mrs. Betty Weiler, school board representative on the committee. Dr. Frank presented a review of the issues he and the school board proposed as the district package. The district proposal included:

(1) a salary increase of 3 percent each year of a two-year contract for all employees in the unit
(2) a reduction in health insurance benefits for part-time employees working twenty to twenty-nine hours per week
(3) a revision of eligibility for fringe benefits from the present fifteen hours per week to twenty hours per week
(4) several minor contract language changes to make the contract conform to present practice.

Mrs. Weiler articulated the board's concern that the cafeteria had been running an increasing deficit for the past three years. Several of the board's proposals addressed the cafeteria deficit problem and the general problem of increasing health costs for all employees. Mrs. Weiler pointed out that the present contract allowed employees working as few as 500 hours per year to be eligible for full fringe benefits. Because most of the cafeteria workers were part-time employees, the benefit costs were inordinate in proportion to salary earned.

Don Garvin listened attentively to the presentation, making notes as Mrs. Weiler and Dr. Frank spoke. When they finished, he addressed the team. "I have some comments and some questions. You are asking some of your employees to give up part of the health insurance benefits they now have, and others to give up eligibility for almost all benefits. Those kinds of rollbacks are difficult, if not impossible, to sell, especially when you offer only a 3 percent salary increase."

Mrs. Weiler responded, "As the board sees it, that is the only way we can bring cafeteria costs into line. We cannot continue to run a deficit in that account. The school cafeteria must pay for itself."

"We have part-time employees other than cafeteria workers who will be affected by these benefit adjustments," added Dr. Frank. "We are looking for substantially reduced costs of benefits. Health insurance costs are going through the ceiling. In checking the records, I found employees who are receiving our family health insurance plan at a value that is greater than the wages they earn."

"How did this get so out of whack?" asked Garvin.

"For one thing, our former superintendent, Jim Burak, could not say no," replied Mrs. Weiler. "He was a hometown boy who grew up with practically all of our nonteaching staff. Then the board made the mistake of listening to Burak and recognizing two units of this group for bargaining purposes. This invited leapfrogging and parity adjustments. I'm afraid now we must face the music and bite the bullet and whatever it is that one must do to regain control."

"How far are you willing to go to accomplish this?" asked Garvin.

"How do you mean that?" inquired Dr. Frank.

"Look, if you want a rollback of the magnitude you're suggesting, you must either buy it with, for example, a more generous salary offer, or use pressure."

"The nonteaching employees in the other association have a contract that calls for a 7 percent salary increase next year. I assume we will eventually offer the same increase to this group," said Dr. Frank. "That should buy something."

"Do you really think so?" demanded Garvin. "That's the kind of logic that got you into this situation. Anyway, I don't believe 7 percent is going to persuade your employees to give up what you are asking."

"Then what will?" asked Mrs. Weiler.

"If you can't put the cafeteria on a pay-as-you-go basis, would you close it?" Garvin replied.

Dr. Frank looked to Betty Weiler for an answer. She just stared back, not knowing what to say. Finally, Dr. Frank volunteered, "I doubt it. Not only would it put a lot of home-town people out of work, but our parents would not stand for it. Where would the kids eat?"

"If you would not close the cafeteria, would you contract for cafeteria services if that was the only way to eliminate the deficit line item?" countered Garvin.

Mrs. Weiler said, "We might consider that. In fact we have talked about it in a general way."

"Then you should propose that the following language be added to Article XIII of the Agreement: 'The District reserves the right to contract or subcontract specific job functions or to join with other districts to provide cafeteria services,' " Garvin stated.

"We are still threatening the jobs of all cafeteria workers in this community," said Dr. Frank. "I would rather propose our original issues as our initial package and see what the reaction is. Why threaten the loss of those jobs if we don't have to? We can always do that."

"I am suggesting a proactive position," responded Garvin. "The troops are divided now and we should take advantage of that."

"I agree," exclaimed Mrs. Weiler. "I think we must threaten something drastic if we expect to be taken seriously. Our part-time school employees get more and better fringe benefits than I do working full time and after twenty years on the job. We are throwing money away. I think the board will go along with Mr. Garvin's suggestion."

Dr. Wayne Frank shrugged his shoulders, giving the palms-up, cave-in sign. "OK—if that's what the board wants, I'll go along with it. I hope you know what you are doing!"

SHATTERED HOPE II

Cindy Robbins, president of the Humbolt Support Staff Group and chief negotiator for the unit, dialed the seven-digit number and waited. "Hello Craig, this is Cindy. I heard you had quite an opening session the other night with the two hired guns blasting away at one another. We have a new ball game in town. From what I hear, the school board is about to set us up. Some of the board members want to create more friction between our two groups. I think we'd better get our negotiating teams together soon. Let's try for Thursday night in the faculty lounge."

DIVIDE AND CONQUER

Questions for Discussion

1. What would you select as the most important factors in this case?

2. How did the benefit package of the part-time employees get so far out of line?
3. Why does Haverquist, the union negotiator, question the board's involvement in the district's proposed negotiation issues?
4. What is your opinion of the way the new superintendent, Dr. Wayne Frank, handled the planning meeting to discuss the district's negotiation proposals and strategies?
5. What is your diagnosis of the whole situation? What went wrong?
6. If you were Mark Haverquist or Cindy Robbins, what issues would you raise at the meeting of the two negotiating committees?

THREE OUT OF FIVE IS NOT A MAJORITY

Negotiator Paul Freeman glanced at the large clock on the boardroom wall. He was surprised to find the large hands set at 3:30 A.M. He stood, stretched, and extended a long arm across the table toward Michael Starr, school board president and district negotiator. Michael reciprocated, and they shook hands.

"A long meeting—well over twelve hours, but worth it," said Paul, smiling. "Can we assume the board's attorney will draw up the revised contract as usual?"

"I don't see why not," replied Michael. He glanced down the table and caught the eye of Mark Wise, school superintendent. "How long will it take you and Jim to come up with a preliminary draft of the contract revisions?"

"I know Jim is in court the next day or two, but we should be able to draft a copy for the teachers to look over within a week," said Mark. "When do you plan to meet with the teachers?"

Paul, president of the Riceville Teachers Association and chief negotiator, conferred with Ben Dalrymple and Frank Harlan, the other two teachers on the negotiating team. "We agree that we want to ratify the contract as soon as we have an approved draft in hand. Some of our teachers are on vacation and probably will be through August. But we would like to have the contract approved before school starts in three weeks, if possible."

"Do you anticipate any problem?" asked Superintendent Wise.

Paul smiled. "No, I don't think so. I think we got pretty much what we expected—in one sense, more. We hoped for a two-year agreement, but we are happy with the three years as proposed and with the salary increments of 10 percent the first year and an average of about 8 percent each of the remaining two years. That in itself should sell it to our members."

"We have a regular board meeting in about a week," said Michael. "I'll have it on the agenda of that meeting."

"Well, that shouldn't be a problem for you, with three of the five board members here tonight, should it?" asked Paul, smiling. "Hey, we proved again that we can do this without hired guns." As he picked up his papers and files to leave the room, Paul failed to notice that Michael did not respond to his question. Had he known what was going through Michael's mind at that moment, he would not have been so confident that a contract was all but signed.

RICEVILLE TOWNSHIP SCHOOL DISTRICT

Riceville Township encompasses the Village of Riceville and a large residential section that serves as a bedroom community for the City of Clarinda to the north. Blue-collar workers employed in Clarinda industries found middle-income homes and building sites in the township. Although the population of the township had more than doubled during the past twenty-five years, some things never seem to change. One of these is the Riceville School Board, which continues to govern with five members, three of whom have been on the board since most people can remember.

Michael Starr is in his twentieth year on the board. During most of that time, he served as president—a position he offered to relinquish when the board asked him to negotiate for the district. His offer was not taken. When the state mandated that all public employers negotiate with employees if requested, the Riceville board proposed to keep the negotiations in-house. The teachers and the support staff agreed, and the parties have successfully negotiated three two-year contracts during the six years since collective bargaining started. The current teacher contract proposal would be the first three-year agreement.

District employees and board members understand that the success of local contract negotiations is in no small measure due to Michael's leadership and integrity. The other board members on the district negotiating committee are Dina Baer, a popular third-term member, and Jess Wooten, the newest member. Jess was elected to a first board term a year ago, upon his retirement as an account executive. He has been active in many community projects, and is well known in the community. Jess ran for the board as the senior citizens' candidate who would hold the line on taxes.

During Mark Wise's interview for the superintendency three years earlier, he was asked his opinion of a board member's negotiating for the school district. He admitted not knowing of any schools that used board negotiators and conceded that the practice was not generally recommended. When told how the board had successfully negotiated contracts with both groups of employees in the past, Mark's comment was, "If it's working, why change it?" During the last negotiation period, Superintendent Wise served as a resource person for both parties and, in the process, facilitated a settlement by suggesting a compromise regarding one of the thornier issues.

RICEVILLE TEACHERS ASSOCIATION

Paul Freeman was elected president of the Riceville Teachers Association the year the association requested recognition as the bargaining agent for the teachers. When the teachers learned that Michael Starr would negotiate for the district, Freeman was asked to negotiate for the association and subsequently was elected president. An active member of the association during his twelve years as a biology teacher at Riceville, he was viewed as a moderate who would get along with Michael Starr. And so he did.

The teachers elected two additional members to serve on the negotiation committee. Ben Dalrymple, a veteran with thirty-eight years' experience as an industrial arts teacher in the district, was elected as an unofficial representative of the senior staff members. Frank Harlan, one of the newest faculty members, was backed and elected by the younger faculty and those who supervised extracurricular activities.

Harlan signed on at Riceville three years ago to teach social studies and coach varsity football. He had a reputation as the most militant of the eighty-four Riceville faculty members.

During the recent negotiations, Harlan opposed the three-year contract because the percentage increment during each of the three years would again give the most money to the highest-paid teachers. He wanted a flat-dollar-amount raise for every teacher each year. The salary compromise called for a 10 percent increment the first year, $2,500 to each teacher the second year, and an 8 percent increment the third year. Harlan was not happy with that arrangement, but supported it when extracurricular salaries were raised 9 percent each year of the three-year contract. The fact that he would gain the most by the percentage arrangement in the case of extracurricular salaries, because he was the highest-paid coach, was not lost on him.

Although the Riceville teachers chose not to use the professional negotiator available through affiliation with their state organization, they did use him as a consultant.

When Paul Freeman informed the consultant of the specific settlements in the tentative agreement, the consultant urged ratification as soon as possible. He told Paul that it was one of the best early agreements heard of in this round of negotiations.

THE IMPASSE

When a week had passed with no word from either the school board or the superintendent about the revised contract document, Freeman called Michael Starr. "Mike, how is Jim coming with the revised contract? I know he had some court cases, but we understood that the revision would get to us within a few days. Our teachers are anxious to have a look at it, and I want to schedule a meeting for that purpose. I don't anticipate a problem, but the sooner we can ratify the agreement, the better."

"I just got off the phone with Mark," responded Mike, "and he told me Jim's law office delivered the contracts this morning. Why don't you pick up several copies at Mark's office? I want to tell you, though, we have a problem. Tom and Robin, our two board members not on the committee, are not happy with the contract. They object to..."

"So what?" Paul interrupted. "The three of you who were there and agreed to the changes we made will just have to convince the others that it's a good contract."

"It's not that simple," Mike replied. "When I talked to Tom and Robin, they had already heard the particulars from Jess. And they say that Jess will not support it now."

"He can't do that!" shouted Paul into the phone. "Jess sat through all the meetings smiling the whole time, seemingly agreeing with all the changes being made in the contract. At the end, he even came up to me to congratulate us on the good job we had done."

"I know," said Mike. "What you don't know is the difficulty I had getting him to go along with the three-year contract. I almost said something to you about Jess after our last meeting, when you assumed this was a wrap-up for the board because three of us were there. I guess I should have. In all fairness to Jess, he did warn us that Tom and Robin would probably not go along with the salaries we were agreeing to, especially on a three-year contract. But I really thought Jess was sold on the package and that he would help us convince the other two. Anyway, we have our meeting tomorrow night, and Dina, Mark, and I plan to work on Jess."

"I'll see if we can schedule a ratification meeting tomorrow night too." said Paul. "You are going to have one demoralized faculty if the contract is not approved on your end. Everyone knows that three board members were present at the meeting, and three is a majority. How will you explain that?"

"There is only one explanation," replied Mike. "The board is not bound by tentative agreements during negotiation, no matter how many members are present. The board must approve the new contract in formal session. And that is what we'll try to do tomorrow night."

"Our teachers' meeting tomorrow, if we can get it scheduled, should be brief. Our negotiation committee unanimously supports the new contract and expects the teachers will do the same. I'll be home after the meeting.

Call me after your board meeting."

"Will do. Our meeting shouldn't run late either, since the new contract is the only major agenda item."

Paul immediately called Ben Dalrymple and Frank Harlan, asking each to set in motion his branch of the faculty telephone calling tree. Within a couple of hours they would know the number of teachers who could attend a meeting the following day. Paul said nothing of his conversation with Mike but suggested that the negotiating committee meet at his house tonight to review the new contract. That would be time enough to let them in on the bad news. He left to drive over to the superintendent's office in the high school building.

He greeted Marcy, the superintendent's secretary, "Hi, I think you have a contract copy for me."

"Hello, Paul. Dr. Wise has your copy and wants to see you. Why don't you go right in."

Paul liked Mark Wise. In his three years as superintendent, Mark had moved forward on much-needed changes. His predecessor, the former superintendent, was of the old school. All important decisions and many of little or minor importance were made by the central office. The staff was informed of the way it was to be. When, on rare occasion, the superintendent was reminded of the many recent proposals calling for more teacher influence and empowerment in decision making, he brushed those notions aside as the latest buzzwords that would soon disappear. Dr. Wise, on the other hand, determined during his first year that the faculty in each of the three school sites was capable of shared decision making, and he initiated a committee system for planning. A number of new projects have been completed by the committees, which were coordinated and supported by the central office. School-site decision making had a toehold at Riceville.

Paul especially appreciated the supporting role Dr. Wise played in the negotiation process. Serving primarily as a source of information and advisor to both parties, Dr. Wise also proved to be an effective mediator. That talent might come in handy again, Paul mused, as he entered the superintendent's office.

"Hi Paul—come in," said Dr. Wise as he stood and emerged from behind his desk so that he and Paul could sit at the small conference table on one side of his office. As he handed Paul copies of the revised agreement, he continued, "I believe this document accurately reflects the changes we agreed to at our last meeting. If you discover any errors as you go through it, please insert corrections on one of the copies and get it back to me. Mike told me he talked to you about our problem."

"Yes, he did, and I am hoping you and Mike can persuade the board to honor the tentative agreement represented by this document," Paul said, pointing to the contract on the table. "I feel confident the teachers will unanimously approve this provisional agreement when given the opportunity. That is why it will be so demoralizing if the board does not ratify it."

"I realize that, but I think you'd better be prepared to face that possibility."

"We have not had this experience before. What happens next? Declaration of impasse?"

"That could be the next step," Dr. Wise replied. "Robin, the most vocal of the board members, insists that we go back to the table and negotiate a one-year contract. She called me when she heard about the contract changes and was livid."

"What's her big problem?" asked Paul. "I don't recall her acting this way during previous negotiations."

"A combination of things, probably," said Mark. "She has had a rough year at the public library. Apparently the library lost one of the major grants it has had and was counting on. Due partly to that, her library board held this year's salary raises to just over 5 percent. Then, when state funding was decreased, the board suggested personnel cuts. At that point she threatened to resign as director. So far, she has not had to let anyone go. Her comment was that the 10 percent we are offering teachers is twice what her workers got, and, in addition, we are committing to almost the same percentage during each of the next two years."

"But the library's problems shouldn't control school board decisions," said Paul angrily.

"That's right, but they do influence her thinking. She has reminded Jess of the special interest group he believes he represents. She has asked him how he will explain those raises and the inevitable tax increases to his senior citizens' group. And that has Jess running scared."

Paul stood up to leave. "Well, let's hope we can work it out. I surely don't want to be a party to our first impasse. Mike is going to call me at home after your meeting tomorrow night."

That evening, when Ben and Frank arrived at Paul's home to review the revised contract document, they reported that more than 90 percent of the teachers could attend the hastily called meeting the next day. That was considered a good number, given that it was the month of August and a few would still be on vacation. The teachers' negotiation team found the contract revisions to be in order. Paul then informed the other two team members of the problem that had developed on the school board.

Frank was furious. "If they don't ratify this contract, I think we should file an improper practice of bad-faith negotiations."

"I took the liberty of calling our state association negotiation representative to get his opinion," said Paul.

"He suggested we proceed with our meeting to ratify the contract. There is nothing else we can do until the school board makes its decision. If they approve the revised document, we have a three-year contract. If they do not accept the proposed agreement, we have several options. Our representative suggested we meet again with their negotiation team to find out specifically what it is they object to."

"We know what they object to—you told us what that pushy broad Robin Williams wants, and we can't accept that!" screamed Frank. "I say we declare impasse."

"What do you think, Ben?" asked Paul. "You've been pretty quiet during all of this."

"I agree with our state association representative to play it cool until we get a definite board decision. If the board turns it down, we have to know the reasons. I say we go ahead with our teachers' meeting tomorrow night and then wait for the board's decision." Ben turned to Frank, shrugged his shoulders, and said, "Sorry, Frank—I can't go along with you."

"Then that's the way we'll play it," said Paul. "At the meeting tomorrow, I'll go over the changes in the new contract and would appreciate having both of you on the dais to help answer questions. As far as I know, the school board's problem has not become public knowledge, and I suggest we keep it that way. Either of you want a beer?"

The next night, Paul watched as the genial group of teachers, obviously on vacation, filed into the school cafeteria. They noisily greeted and welcomed one another, for many had not seen the others during the summer vacation. Their demeanor clearly indicated that they had heard about the new contract but had not learned about the board problem. The association secretary signaled Paul that almost all the teachers were present, so he called the meeting to order and began to address the group.

Contract changes that improved the lot of the teachers were greeted with cheers and clapping. The loss of association contract proposals through negotiation and the several board proposals accepted by the association team were accepted quietly, with only a few questions for clarification.

As the discussion progressed, the teachers as a group sensed that, overall, they were hearing the outline of a very favorable contract. After the last issue was presented and discussed and Paul asked for any last questions, the teachers rose and gave the negotiating team a standing ovation. Many teachers came up to personally congratulate the members of the team and to comment on "a job well done." The new contract was approved without a dissenting vote.

At 10:50 P.M., the phone in Paul's den interrupted the heated discussion that he, Ben, and Frank were having concerning the probability of the Buffalo Bills' getting into the Super Bowl. All three were rabid fans. Paul picked up the phone and nodded to his colleagues, signaling that it was Michael Starr on the other end. He told Mike that the teachers had unanimously approved the contract and said that he wanted to turn on his speakerphone so Ben and Frank could hear the rest of the conversation.

Mike said, "OK," and then proceeded to tell them about the board meeting. "The board did not approve the contract as revised at the last negotiation meeting, primarily because of the three-year term combined with the overall salary increment of 26 percent over the three years. The board's decision was on a split vote. After much discussion, the board was willing to honor the 10 percent salary increase on a one-year contract or would consider a multiyear contract with reduced percentage increases. We don't expect an answer tonight. The board suggests the two negotiating committees get together to discuss the issues once again. Perhaps other alternatives are possible."

Silence.

Finally, Paul said, "We are very disappointed, as will be our association members. Of course, we will not give an answer tonight. You will hear from us when we have made a decision."

"I'm sorry people—I wish we could have followed your example. I'll look forward to hearing from you...I think.

Goodnight."

"Now will you listen to me?" asked Frank after Paul hung up the phone.

Paul spoke, "I have given this situation a great deal of thought the last couple of days, and this is what I think we should do...."

THREE OUT OF FIVE IS NOT A MAJORITY

Questions for Discussion

1. What basic issues does this case pose for you?
2. How might Michael Starr, board negotiator, have handled things differently?
3. How should one deal with board members like Jess Wooten?

4. What factors influenced Dina Baer to take the position she did regarding the contract?
5. What does this case say for board members' serving as negotiators?
6. If you were Paul Freeman, what action would you recommend to the association members?

THE NAIVE TOWN SUPERVISOR

Tom Brighton steered his rusting, ten-year-old pickup into the one vacant parking space behind the wood-frame town hall. He recognized the two cars in the only other spaces on the dirt lot. The new LTD Crown Victoria belonged to David Erickson, the recently elected Sanborn town supervisor. The red Horizon told him that Susan Quinn, part-time town clerk, was also working today. When Susan had called, she could not tell Tom why Mr. Erickson wanted to meet with him right away. Of one thing Tom was sure. The meeting would aggravate the growing hostility between the new supervisor and the union that Tom was president of. Tom decided to have one last smoke before going in to face the anticipated confrontation. He lit a cigarette and thought to himself, David Erickson has heard we joined the Teamsters. Well, he asked for it.

A CASE OF PAST PRACTICE

Relations between the bargaining unit and the new town supervisor began to take a turn for the worse shortly after David Erickson's election in January. For years, the town had had a practice of hiring seasonal employees from June through August each year to cover vacation periods of workers in the sanitation and highway departments. By agreement between the local bargaining unit and the town, the seasonal workers were not included in the blue-collar unit. In addition, because highway workers were paid a higher rate, seasonals had been assigned to sanitation work. This allowed regular sanitation employees to be released temporarily to fill the higher-paid positions of vacationing highway workers.

In January, within several weeks of David Erickson's election as town supervisor, he began hiring seasonal workers to begin immediately as assigned members of the highway department. The local union petitioned to open negotiations to include the seasonals as members of the bargaining unit. When the town refused to negotiate the issue, the union filed a grievance.

Before the assignment of an arbitrator by the State Public Employment Relations Board, Tom Brighton called the town supervisor. "David, why don't we get together and see if we can iron this thing out."

"Are you worried that the union will lose if we get to arbitration?" asked David.

"Quite the contrary," responded Tom. "I am certain the town will lose the case. But each side will lose in the sense that we share the cost of arbitration when maybe we can settle it without that cost. And then there is the satisfaction of settling it ourselves."

"Tell me how we breached the contract by what we did. Seasonal employees are not mentioned."

"That's true," said Tom, "but our practice of using the seasonal employees was generally agreed to by both parties for a good many years—for more years than you have lived in this community."

"Well, I'm willing to let an arbitrator decide this issue. We must reserve the right to assign our employees where we want."

"You will lose on this one," warned Tom. "Just remember we offered to try to settle this without arbitration."

During arbitration, David Erickson, representing the town, argued that the contract had not been violated, nor had past practice been changed. Because the union had agreed to exclude the seasonal workers from the unit, the assignment and work of these laborers had never been reserved for unit employees. In addition, no unit employees had lost their jobs as a result of the action.

The unit representative, Tom Brighton, argued that the hiring of seasonal nonunit employees had, by past practice, been limited to vacation periods and to lower-paying positions. Thus, it was improper for the town to unilaterally violate that limitation.

The arbitrator ruled in favor of the union.

"It is irrelevant," he said, "that no unit employees were laid off." Referring to another case, he cited, "A public employer may not assign tasks of unit employees to nonunit employees unless the tasks or the qualifications for the job have been substantially changed."

David Erickson was livid.

Two days after receiving the arbitrator's award, David called Tom to his office. "We have informed the seasonal employees that they are out of a job due to your grievance. We may be hiring them again in June. I also want to warn you that this issue will be top priority on our agenda during the next round of negotiations. We have not given up on this."

"You mean *you* haven't given up on this," responded Tom. "Other members of the town board are not happy with your handling of this case. Why would they want to make a big case out of an issue that had not been a problem until you took charge?"

"Just be ready for some tough negotiations," warned David.

At a special union meeting, Tom informed the unit members of this conversation and recommended affiliation with the state union organization. He expressed specific interest in one of the benefits of such an alliance—the service of a professional negotiator. Tom explained that his effectiveness as the union negotiator had been drastically reduced by the supervisor's hostility. Either another member of the local union should take over as negotiator, or a "hired gun" should be brought in.

Several union members spoke in favor of Tom's suggestion to join the state Teamsters. Others were skeptical.

"How much would our dues increase?" asked one member.

"I don't know," responded Tom. "I talked to Barry Hughes, the Teamsters' area representative, who would like to meet with us to discuss the situation. He claims our economic gains over the next few years will more than make up for the increased dues. I think we ought to listen to him."

"But how will Dave Erickson react when he hears we have an outside negotiator?" asked one highway employee.

"He will not like it," responded Tom.

"Won't that make it harder than ever to deal with him?" asked another member.

"It might," replied Tom. "I have the feeling he took a hard line with me because he thought he could intimidate me. I doubt he expected us to take the seasonal worker issue to arbitration. Several times I suggested we settle this issue by ourselves. I also think he is so naive that he did not understand the issues involved with the seasonal workers. He really believed he could win in arbitration."

"What do you think will happen if we join the Teamsters and become Local 10988?"

"I won't have to negotiate," said Tom. Changing the subject, he asked, "Well, how about it—shall we have Barry Hughes meet with us?"

Two weeks later, Barry Hughes met with the local union members to discuss affiliation with the Teamsters. The next day, Tom Brighton began his campaign for a representative election. A month later, the officers of the local union presented a petition, signed by all members, requesting the town board to recognize their affiliation as Teamsters Local 10988 for the purpose of collective bargaining.

COUNTERSTROKE

Tom took one last deep drag on his cigarette, flipped the butt out onto the driveway, and opened the back door of the town hall.

One of the new supervisor's first official acts was to ban all smoking in the small town hall offices. Thus, it was with a perverse pleasure and a grin on his face that he entered the clerk's office exhaling a white cloud of cigarette smoke. Susan looked up smiling, and shook her finger at him, asking, "Are you trying to get me into trouble?" Pointing to the next office, she continued, "Mr. Erickson will smell that through these paper walls."

"Why do you call him 'Mr. Erickson'?" Tom asked. "You called him 'David' when he was only a town board member, and you always called our former supervisor 'Gary.'"

"Who cares? Now he wants to be called 'Mr. Erickson.' I'll let him know you are here."

Through the open door Tom heard David say, "Oh, thanks Susan—send him in. Would you also come in with your notebook?"

Seated in the uncomfortable straight-back wooden chairs, Tom and Susan waited while David continued to scribble something on a clipboard balanced near the edge of the huge oak table between them. Tom had the feeling that he was back in the principal's office at Sanborn High.

After a few minutes, David looked up at Tom. "I asked Susan to make notes of this meeting as a matter of record. Is that OK with you?"

"I don't know. I don't even know what this meeting is all about. When Susan called, she said she couldn't tell me why you wanted to see me. She said she didn't know."

"I want to talk to you about the employees' lunchroom and restroom in the maintenance building. It is my understanding that cleaning these rooms is not a regular part of anyone's job duties. Is that correct?"

"Yes, those who use the rooms are expected to pick up and help keep them clean," responded Tom. Here it comes, he thought.

"Well, that is not happening," said David. "During my visits to the maintenance building, I couldn't help noticing the intolerable condition of these two rooms. Litter and trash can be found on the tables and floor; and the restroom doesn't look as though it is cleaned by sanitation workers."

"Sometimes the men get in a hurry," Tom began to explain, "and they don't clean it all up."

"Because no one is responsible to see that it is cleaned every day," lectured David. "That is what I want you to do."

"You want me to set up a schedule for the men?" asked Tom. He knew better but thought he would give it a try.

"No, I expect you, personally, to keep those rooms clean," said David.

"That is not part of the job description of a sanitation worker," said Tom.

"That's not the point!" shouted David. "I am directing you to clean those rooms or face suspension for insubordination."

"So, is this how I'm to be punished for my activities organizing the successful Teamsters representative election? I thought you would have learned something from the recent past practice case. As president of the union, I had to challenge you on that one. We warned you. We thought you pushed the case because you didn't know any better, and you wouldn't listen. Now you are about to make another dumb mistake by giving me permanent KP. You'll lose again."

"With your disciplinary record, I'm willing to risk that."

THE NAIVE TOWN SUPERVISOR

Questions for Discussion

1. What are the major issues in this case?
2. Why do you think David Erickson refused to discuss the initial problem with Tom Brighton?
3. Why did Erickson insist on "assigning employees where we want"?
4. Do you agree with the arbitrator's ruling? Why or why not?
5. What needs to be done to improve the relationship between the parties in this case?
6. What are the advantages and disadvantages of the supervisor's negotiating for management?
7. If you were Tom Brighton, would you file a grievance for having been assigned "housekeeping" duty?
8. Could issues similar to those in this case emerge during school district negotiations?

THE PRINCIPAL'S
REVOLVING DOOR

"In my book, you're one dumb, unprincipled schnook. How can you seriously consider negotiating for your district against your own faculty?" demanded Phil Roder, Sidney High School principal. Phil's face was flushed, his jaw clenched. He stared angrily at Terry Heath, looking for an answer. The other principals around the table waited expectantly.

TERRY HEATH, PRINCIPAL

Terry Heath is principal of Winterset Junior-Senior High School. Before his appointment six years ago, he taught history in the district for three years. He had no previous teaching experience, having accepted the Winterset history position in the same month he received his master's degree. Terry is an example of a born teacher, if there is such a thing. He relishes the challenge of motivating students to learn history. His enthusiasm for the subject and his creative teaching methods earned him the reputation of being one of the best teachers in the system.

By the end of his third year of teaching, Terry had completed enough graduate hours in administration to receive certification as a secondary school principal. When the high school principal resigned to take a similar position in a larger school district, Terry was offered the job. The salary increase that came with the principalship proved a strong incentive. John Radner, principal of the elementary school, encouraged Terry to take the position. They had become close personal friends during the previous year. Terry accepted with the understanding that he would teach at least one history course a year.

PROBLEMS IN WINTERSET

The Winterset School District has approximately 825 students K–12. Winterset Junior-Senior High School is connected by a breezeway to the Beckwith Elementary School (named for a former school board member). The district's attractive campus borders the north edge of the Village of Winterset. The village posts a population of 1,450 on the sign along the highway leading into town.

Terry's first year as principal went smoothly. Although some teachers thought the principalship should have been offered to a person with more teaching, if not administrative, experience, most of the faculty supported Terry. They liked the idea of a teaching principal. In fact, Dr. Earl Roulea, Winterset superintendent, was heard to say that he was thinking of teaching a class the next year.

During Terry's second year as principal, the state legislature mandated collective bargaining for all public employees. Negotiations were to begin the next year for a contract effective the following year.

The Winterset school board asked the superintendent to negotiate for the district that first year. Dr. Roulea met with the president of the teachers' association to discuss the new procedure. They agreed to meet and discuss, as they had in the past, salary and working conditions. The teachers' negotiation committee resisted pressure from the state association to have a state association representative negotiate for the teachers. After the third bargaining session, the Winterset School District and the Winterset Teachers Association signed a one-year contract. Both principals were offered the same percentage salary increase and increased benefits that the members of the new teachers' union received.

Early in the year of the first contract, the Winterset teachers showed signs of dissatisfaction and uneasiness with the results of that bargaining experience. Discussions in the faculty lounge often revolved around questions such as "Did you hear about the big raises negotiated by the Warren Springs teachers?" and "Why didn't our negotiating committee push for a sick leave bank as the Hastings teachers did?" By the end of the fall semester, the bulletin board in the faculty lounge had a listing of the major teacher contract settlements, including salary, in the three-county area.

In January, the Winterset Teachers Association informed the superintendent that a representative of the state association would represent the local teachers when negotiations started again in March. Superintendent Roulea advised the school board to hire a professional negotiator. The board expressed a vote of confidence in the superintendent and directed him to begin preparing for the next round of bargaining.

The association proposal included thirty-eight issues. The new president of the Winterset association announced that the teachers had a lot of catching up to do. After the sixth bargaining session, the association declared impasse and requested mediation service from the State Public Employment Relations Board.

The new school year started without a new contract and with the process at a standstill. The superintendent recommended that the board accept the recommendations submitted by the fact finder. The board declined, primarily because of a two-year contract provision that the fact finder recommended. One board member also announced publicly, "The teachers' association must ratify the report first." The school board president called a meeting of both negotiation teams on November 15 and announced that any agreement signed after Thanksgiving would not be retroactive. Two days later, the association voted to accept the fact finder's recommendations, amid much grumbling. The board ratified the agreement at a special meeting the next evening.

On the first day of school after Thanksgiving vacation, the superintendent asked the two building principals to meet with him at 4 P.M. "I waited until now to talk to you about your contracts because I thought I could persuade the board to reconsider a decision made at its last meeting. We administrators will receive a 3 percent salary increase plus the fringe increases the other employees received."

"But that's less than half of the percentage increase the others received," protested John Radner.

"I'm aware of that," said Superintendent Roulea. "The board is not pleased with the way negotiations went this year. Most of the members believe our contract settlements were too high, even though they approved the agreement. The board says there is little money left for our raises. Some of the board members blame me, and I'm afraid you are caught in that squeeze."

"We were never involved in negotiation. We were not even asked to comment on the district's issues," said Terry. "The teachers have a two-year contract. What happens to us that second year? Do we take what they give us—maybe nothing?"

"Terry, I think you and I should ask for unit recognition and start negotiating with the district," said John. "Both the State School Administrators Association and the State Federation of School Administrators are looking for members."

"I hope it doesn't come to that," said Superintendent Roulea. "I look upon us as an administrative team, and that would change if you requested negotiation, at least in the minds of board members.

"Earl, I don't mean to be disrespectful, but I take exception to your concept of administrative team," said Radner. "I have been a principal here in Winterset for twelve years, and I have never felt part of an administrative team. This is especially true during these critical years of negotiation. I have never been consulted about negotiations with the employee units in my building. I have not been asked to analyze the current contract nor the proposed contract for building-level implications. Terry and I suggested that we ought to be consulted. It has not happened."

"The board did not want you principals involved in bargaining. They believed it would only confuse the process," said Earl. He then changed the subject. "I don't know what will happen during the next round of negotiations. I'm sure I will not be doing it again. Maybe now they'll take my suggestion and hire a professional negotiator." He turned toward the window to watch the children on the playground. The meeting was over.

Terry and John agreed that during the summer they would contact both state administrators' organizations about forming a bargaining unit. Neither of them did.

During the next school year, Superintendent Roulea and the building committee of the board concentrated on the major building project approved by the district voters in the last election. With the superintendent traveling much of the time, interviewing contractors and inspecting recent school constructions, the two principals assumed the authority, which had never been delegated, to manage their schools. The school board president requested that the principals attend the monthly board meetings. This policy change gave hope. Did this mean full membership on the administrative team? The answer was not long in coming. Discussions at these meetings led the principals to perceive that the board was floundering for lack of administrative leadership. Hearsay, gossip, and rumors all too often formed the basis for evaluations of school personnel and policy decisions. Superintendent Roulea's indecisiveness and straddling of issues led the board president to appropriate many executive functions. Thus, it was the board president who suggested that the two district principals represent the district in the coming negotiations with district employees. "You have a good relationship with the teachers, and we have to mend some fences," he explained.

During the summer, Terry and John weighed the pros and cons of that offer. They had given up the idea of forming an administrators' bargaining unit.

THE CORNER CONFERENCE EXECUTIVE MEETING

Ten school districts in the southwestern area of the state with comparable student enrollment form the Corner Conference. The Corner Conference provides a medium for the exchange of athletic and cultural activities among the member schools. One elementary and one secondary principal from each member district serve on the Conference Board, which governs the organization. Five members of the Conference Board serve on an executive committee, which meets periodically to plan the agenda for Conference Board meetings. It was at the September meeting of the executive committee that Phil Roder confronted Terry Heath about the rumor that he and John Radner would negotiate for the school district.

Gary Bunkers, elementary principal in the Alton School District, broke the silence, "Come on Phil—lighten up. Terry hasn't said that he would negotiate. He said they were considering it."

"Anyway, is it any of our business?" asked Joel Fisher, Warren Springs High School principal.

Terry glared at Phil, jaws clenched. "No it isn't, but I want to explain something. John and I feel that we are losing ground at Winterset. The teachers and the support staff negotiate, which gives them some control over salary and working conditions. John and I don't even have that. Our superintendent is in trouble with the board and is not about to further jeopardize his position by advocating equal treatment for administration. At this point, I think he will stay in Winterset no matter what the board offers him. He is buying time to find another position. He admitted to us that we were 'caught in the squeeze,' as he put it. John and I talked about requesting recognition as a bargaining unit. At about this time, the board asked us to negotiate for the district. We said we'd think about it, and that is what we're doing."

"But why would you even think about it?" demanded Phil.

"What do you hope to gain?" inquired Dan Weber, Hastings Elementary School principal and fifth member of the executive committee.

Terry elected to answer Dan. "We're not sure. On the other hand, what do we have to lose? Right now John and I consider ourselves in a state of suspended animation. We have no idea what our standing is with the board, or with the superintendent for that matter. The school board's primary employee concern is to get the best possible contract with the two unions without big waves. Board members feel the superintendent failed to do that. Now they have asked us to try. If we succeed, and we think we can, we become an integral part of the management team."

"But, to get back to Phil's question," said Dan, "how will that affect your relationship with teachers and other employees in your building?"

"We will have to work harder to maintain a professional relationship," replied Terry. "I think teachers consider principals managers and administration. Why else are they and their unions so intent on teacher empowerment and getting involved in decision making?"

"All the more reason not to get involved in the bargaining process," said Phil. "You'll not promote collegiality with your staff by negotiating against them."

"I don't think collegiality has anything to do with it," responded Terry. "You tell me what's collegial about recent developments in Taylors Falls and Chicago."

"What?"

"The Taylors Falls School District in Minnesota replaced the principal with an elected group of five teachers. The teacher team will serve as building administration. Team teachers will continue teaching full time and will each receive $800 for administrative responsibilities. Other small districts are monitoring this arrangement. We are not indispensable.

"Under a new Illinois state law, half of Chicago's principals will lose their tenure in 1990, and half in 1991. Each school will form a council to select replacements. The council will be made up of at least six parents, two teachers, and two community members. Oh, by the way, principals not retained by their school's council may be placed on an eligibility list for consideration when a teacher vacancy occurs."

"What if there isn't a vacancy in their field?" asked Dan.

"They lost their tenure, so I assume they're out," answered Joel.

"Those are two extreme cases," said Phil. "Rochester, New York, is a more representative example of what's happening with teacher empowerment. There, planning teams of teachers and administrators have the authority to make school-level decisions about teacher selection, scheduling, and staff development activities, among others. Principals will serve as resource persons and the resident experts on the building planning teams. Under this arrangement, principals could not possibly negotiate for the school district with the teachers' association. And I believe this is the direction in which we are headed."

"Anyone know how the Rochester principals view the new contract?" asked Gary.

"One article I read recently in *Educational Leadership* indicates that Rochester principals who took part in a survey supported the idea of collegiality," replied Terry.

"This is all so confusing to me," said Dan Weber, the youngest principal in the group. "I know the American Federation of Teachers is supporting the Rochester plan and contract. Yet, I read recently that the American Federation of School Administrators, which is also affiliated with the AFL-CIO, has filed a grievance against the American Federation of Teachers in an effort to stop AFT support of efforts to turn over to teachers responsibilities traditionally held by principals."

"It really is confusing," agreed Terry, "and that is why John and I are weighing other options. One option I'm considering is to just get out and go back to full-time teaching. I would rather leave at a time of my own choosing than be voted out later. I have less time in administration than any of you except Dan, and I already feel burned out. It's probably frustration more than anything else. I read about all the Band-Aid education reform measures passed by state legislatures and state education departments and wonder how they will eventually affect me. Right now, it seems to me the most dangerous and vulnerable place to be is in neutral territory, and that's where I consider the principalship to be. We are quasi-administrators pretending to be members of a teaching profession. Hell—in Winterset it's worse. Our superintendent thinks John and I are part of a management team. And the teachers know we're not. Now the board wants to give us a shot at it, and we don't know what to do."

"If you're worried about power and maintaining your place in the educational structure, my advice is to seek unit recognition and negotiate your principals' contract with the district," said Gary.

"Maybe that's what we will do," replied Terry. "In any event, this group is not going to solve our problem. Let's get on with the conference agenda."

THE DECISION

Terry parked his car in the reserved slot marked *Principal* on the school parking lot. As he walked toward Winterset High School and his office, he wondered how many more times he would park his car in that particular place. After greeting Terry, his secretary said that Superintendent Roulea had called several times and asked that Terry call him as soon as he came in. Seated at his desk, Terry glanced at the mail that had accumulated on the desk, pushed it aside, and decided to get it over with. He dialed the superintendent's office.

"Hello, Earl. I thought I'd call and tell you, in advance of the board meeting tonight, the decision John and I have made regarding the negotiation proposal."

THE PRINCIPAL'S REVOLVING DOOR

Questions for Discussion

1. What questions does this case pose for you?
2. To what extent should principals be consulted during negotiations with other employee units in their buildings?
3. Why should principals have the opportunity to analyze the current contract and the proposed contract for building-level implications?
4. Generally, in schools today, is the concept of "management team" working?
5. To what extent should principals feel threatened by the reforms that give teachers new status?
6. Do you agree with Terry in assuming that if he and John succeed in negotiations they will become an integral part of the management team?
7. What would your decision be if you were Terry or John?

THE MEDDLING MIDDLE MANAGERS

Vincent Dillon picked up the phone on the fifth ring, remembering that his secretary, Nancy, was out of the office on an errand for him. "Superintendent Dillon's office," he said.

"Vince, I'm glad I caught you before you left. This is Christine." Vincent recognized the voice. He ought to. Christine Clements, as president of the Middleton Board of Education, is in touch with Middleton's Superintendent of Schools almost daily. She is publisher and editor of the *Middleton County Times*, the only local daily newspaper serving the area.

"Christine, what can I do for you?" he asked.

"One of my reporters, Clair Jones, just received a call from Sidney Ames. He and the other principals are meeting tonight to consider a vote to strike. I don't know why you let this happen. We all know teachers threaten to strike. But who ever heard of principals going on strike? Is that possible?"

Rendered speechless, Vincent thought for a moment. "No, I don't think so," he replied unconvincingly. "But let me check it out and get back to you." With that he quickly hung up the phone before Christine could ask more questions. Damn! I can't believe they would actually strike, he said to himself. He needed answers. While dialing the high school principal's number, he continued muttering to himself. Well, I can't say I wasn't warned!

THE MIDDLETON COUNTY SCHOOL DISTRICT

The Middleton County School District came into being five years ago when the four independent Middleton County school districts merged to form one district. The consolidation was the result of a long, and often bitter, school reorganization effort. Two independent districts, Linton and Bryant, were pressured by the state to merge because of low enrollments. Rushford, the largest town and school district in the county, agreed to join the group provided that Marion, the fourth independent district, agreed to become a member of the reorganized county school system.

The new county district constructed a new comprehensive high school building in Rushford and a new middle school in each of the Towns of Marion and Bryant. Five elementary schools—two in Rushford and one in each of the other three towns in the county—round out the new district's learning centers. The central administration's Offices of the Superintendent, Assistant Superintendent for Instruction, and Business Manager are located in the renovated former Rushford High School building. Each of the elementary and middle schools has a full-time building principal. The high school principal and an assistant principal administer the comprehensive secondary school.

During reorganization discussions, a very sensitive and heated issue was the administrative organization of the new district and who would fill those positions. Each of the four former independent districts had a superintendent and two building principals—one elementary and one secondary. The administrative chart for the new district kept the number of administrators at twelve, but with a different mix. The new district school board moved quickly to select Dr. Vincent Dillon, former Rushford superintendent, as chief school officer of the Middleton County School District. The former superintendent of Marion Independent Schools became the assistant superintendent. George Durkin, the former Linton superintendent, applied for both superintendents' positions. He received neither. Instead, he was offered the high school principalship, which he grudgingly accepted. Thus, Sidney Ames, Rushford's former high school principal, lost the position he felt rightly belonged to him. When he was offered the assistant principalship of the new high school, he turned it down and applied for the principalship of one of the middle schools. Several administrators, including the former Bryant superintendent, elected to move on to other districts.

Reorganization was not as traumatic for the teachers in the four former independent districts. A general agreement was made with the teachers' associations that no teacher currently under contract would lose his or her job as a result of the reorganization. Longevity would be considered when teachers had to be reassigned to other schools and positions. Planned retirements and voluntary leaves over periods of two to three years would adjust the teacher force to acceptable levels.

The reorganized school board honored the commitments made to the teachers' groups during the many consolidation discussions. The new negotiated teacher contract provided salary adjustments for all teachers who made less than Rushford teachers with comparable experience and education. Rushford had the best salary schedule in the county. The new salary schedule included a 10 percent salary adjustment the first year and an 8 percent increase each subsequent year of the three-year contract. The lowest-paid teachers in the county received 20 to 30 percent salary increase the first year. In addition, the new contract improved many fringe benefits and other working conditions for most teachers.

The Middleton consolidation was not as accommodating and advantageous to the administrators of the four former independent districts who elected to remain in the system. The four independent districts did not have bargaining agreements with administrators. The number of superintendent positions was cut from four to two—one chief executive officer and an assistant. Although the number of building principal positions remained the same, reorganization eliminated three high schools and added two middle schools. None of the principals in the four former independent districts had middle school experience.

George Durkin, the former Linton superintendent, informally accused the Middleton County School Board of going back on its word and asked for a hearing. He claimed that during the reorganization discussions the board declared that all qualified candidates would be given fair and equal consideration for the superintendency. This was not the case, charged George Durkin, because Vince Dillon was handpicked by the board from the very beginning. The board tried unsuccessfully to reassure him that he and the other candidates were seriously considered for the position.

THE MIDDLE MANAGERS ORGANIZE

In May of the new district's first year, Superintendent Dillon sent notice to the district's principals of a 5 percent salary increase approved by the board for administrators. Several weeks later, Dr. Dillon received a copy of a memo to all principals from George Durkin calling a meeting to discuss organization of a bargaining unit. Vincent Dillon was livid. He asked his secretary to set up a meeting with Principal Durkin as soon as possible. It was scheduled for 9:00 A.M. the next day.

Dr. Dillon wasted no time getting to the point. "Why did I have to learn from a memo of your intent to incite our principals to form a bargaining unit?"

"In the first place, I am not inciting anything!" shot back George. "I was asked to call the meeting to discuss a bargaining unit. In the second place, we are not seeking permission to bargain; we have that right. I sent you a copy of the memo as a courtesy, to give you advance notice of what we intend to do."

"I can't believe the principals are serious about negotiating with the board," said Superintendent Dillon. "They are a part of the management team, not a labor union. As a former superintendent of schools, you should realize that."

"I used to think so," responded George. "When we were small rural districts, principals could count on informal, good relations with the superintendent and board members. Principals wielded influence because they could be heard and get results."

"And you think that is not happening now?" asked Dr. Dillon.

"I do," replied George. "Most of us are not happy with present conditions. We believe you and the board favored the teachers' group during the reorganization process, especially in setting and adjusting salaries. You had to negotiate with them. Teachers received a 10 percent raise this year and will get an 8 percent raise next year. Principals will receive another 5 percent increase per your memo to us. We were not even consulted. You will have to talk to us about raises if you have to negotiate with us."

Dr. Dillon pushed his chair back from the desk and walked over to the bay window facing the concourse between buildings. "You know your petition to be recognized as a negotiating unit is an indirect criticism of me?"

"You *and* the school board," corrected George.

"The board members will not see it that way. To them it implies that I have not been able to forge a working management team. Now part of that team wants to negotiate with the board. This move will only complicate matters."

"We hope not. We believe it will force the school board and you to discuss middle management working conditions with us. By exercising our right to negotiate with the board, we will be heard."

"I can see that I'm not going to change your mind," said Dr. Dillon. "I want you to know that I plan to talk to the other principals about this."

"That's fine with me. I will let you know when we have made a decision."

Two weeks later, Christine Clements, president of the Middleton Board of Education, received a letter from George Durkin, president of the Middleton Middle Management Association (MMMA), requesting recognition for the purpose of collective bargaining. The letter also announced that George Durkin would negotiate for the association and asked the board of education to suggest several dates for an initial meeting. Christine Clements insisted that Dr. Dillon represent the district in negotiations with the MMMA. She had not altered her initial belief that he was responsible for what she called the principals' mutiny. Now let him deal with it, she thought to herself.

Negotiations between the MMMA and the district got off to a bad start. In his opening statement, George Durkin claimed that the district had broken promises and played favorites in setting personnel salaries during reorganization. The district charged that several MMMA members had collected retirement incentives and then decided not to retire, thereby breaking an agreement.

Having arrived at the point of negotiation, the MMMA demanded a 19 percent salary increase during the first year of a three-year contract, with an additional 9 percent each subsequent year. The MMMA argued that substantial salary increases were warranted because of the modest raises provided during recent years. The board insisted on a one-year contract with a 5 percent increase. The board claimed that its offer was fair because one does not spend percentages but rather real dollars; and, at 5 percent, principals get more dollars than most teachers get at 9 percent.

Personality conflicts, unreasonable attitudes, and inflexible positions on the part of both parties made impasse inevitable. The state-assigned mediator was unable to bring the parties to agreement. A fact finder was assigned. The fact finder's recommendations were not acceptable to either party but served as a basis for further negotiations. The final two-year agreement included an annual salary increase of 9 percent. In addition, the MMMA gained an accrued-sick-leave buyout plan, a grievance procedure, and a sabbatical leave plan—all top-priority issues. Although the district board ratified the contract, many board members felt the district had conceded too much and received too little in return.

In the third year of consolidation, the Middleton Teachers Association and the district began negotiating a successor agreement to the one that would expire on June 30. Sensing the tension and dissension within administrative ranks, the association set out to capture a bigger share of the decision-making process. Issues limiting the power of the building principals moved up on the list of priorities. As a prelude, with negotiations barely under way, the association initiated a confrontation over a school principal's right to evaluate teachers. The association targeted the new high school, where teacher militancy was the strongest. The association's Building Committee advised George Durkin that he must hereafter give advance notice to any teacher before attempting either a formal or informal classroom visit. But contract language said, "The Principal shall be responsible for the evaluation of classroom teachers. The purpose of teacher evaluation is the improvement of instruction."

For two years, George had struggled to understand the many facets of the teacher contract that had never been clarified by central administration. But this clause seemed clear to him. He notified the association that he intended to evaluate teachers as he had in the past. After his next unannounced classroom visit, the association filed a grievance. As management's frontline representative, George held to his decision. The grievance was then appealed to the superintendent, who preferred not to field grievances. Thus, at one point during teacher–school board negotiations, Dr. Dillon suggested that the grievance be dropped because that issue was on the table as a bargaining chip. The association, having made its point, agreed.

THE STRAW THAT BROKE THE...

Sidney Ames maneuvered his car into the first vacant reserved slot he found behind the high school building. As he closed the car door, a familiar voice emerged from among the parked vehicles, "Hey, Sid, are you lost?"

Sidney glanced around to find the friendly person of Don Sand coming toward him. "No more lost than usual," he replied with a grin. He liked Don, who had been football coach at Rushford High during Sidney's years as principal. Sand had been appointed athletic director and head football coach of the reorganized Middleton district. Since Sidney assumed the principalship of the middle school, he had not seen as much of Don as he would have liked. They had worked well together.

"I'm here to see George," Sidney continued. "Apparently he has information about the new teacher contract. He sounded very upset when he called me."

"Yes, I know," said Don. "I am the one who told him about the proposed contract. The teachers' negotiating committee called a meeting last night to sound out the membership on progress to date. I couldn't believe some of the things the board and Dillon are willing to concede. I'm a teacher now, but someday soon I want to move into a principalship. If I were an administrator, I would be concerned about this contract. When I mentioned this to George this morning, he didn't know much about anything. George is OK to work for, but I'd rather work with you. You should have had the high school principalship. George always seems so depressed."

"Principals are not involved in teacher contract negotiations," Sidney said, ignoring the personal comments about George. "Ever since we formed our bargaining unit, and even before that, the board more or less ignored us. I'd better get in there; George is waiting. Nice seeing you again."

"If this is the way it's going to be, I may change my mind about finishing my administration certification program." Don waved and moved on toward his car.

George was waiting impatiently in his office. "I saw you talking to Don in the parking lot, so I assume you know why I called you."

"Actually, Don didn't give me any details. He said he told you about some very disturbing issues being discussed by the board and teachers' association," said Sidney.

"After talking to Don this morning," George continued, "I visited with several other teachers who were willing to talk about their contract. They confirmed what Don told me. If the board approves all of the issues still on the table, as I'm informed they could, building principals are going to be in trouble. For example, one proposal provides that any teacher who is assigned a physically handicapped student shall be relieved from all noninstructional responsibilities, such as bus duty, cafeteria supervision, study hall, and hall duty."

"How are we going to implement that one?" asked Sidney.

"I have no idea, but listen to some of the others. One proposal restricts teachers' meetings called by building principals to one hour per month. Another mandates that every teacher have a forty-five-minute daily preparation period. Another that I can't live with unless I get more staff limits assignment of high school teachers to classes involving no more than three preparations."

"Where in the hell does Dillon stand on all of this?" asked Sidney. "He must know how difficult it will be to implement these. I can't believe the district will approve these issues without asking us about them."

"Have you been asked? Were you aware that these issues were under consideration?"

"Yes and no; I heard a few rumors, but I didn't take them seriously. It appears I should have. No, I have not been consulted about proposed teacher contract changes."

"The teachers I talked to today believe that the board is ready to tentatively approve the contract that calls for the changes I mentioned, and of course others," said George. "Apparently, the teachers' association is willing to buy some priority proposals by conceding economic issues. Money speaks!"

"We'd better set up a meeting of all building principals with Dr. Dillon to discuss this before it is too late," suggested Sidney.

"I already tried that. After my meeting with Don this morning, I called Dillon to ask him about some of the concerns I'll have if the teacher contract is ratified. He said he didn't want to discuss the subject over the phone. When I asked for an appointment, he put me off. I proposed that he meet with the principals to hear our views on the contract. He suggested we stop meddling in teacher bargaining and concentrate on our own bargaining problems."

"My God—can he really be that insensitive to the impact of such a contract?" asked Sidney.

"It appears so. I gave notice that the principals could not just stand by and allow the board to approve that contract without an opportunity to comment. I asked to be placed on the agenda of the next board meeting in order to present our concerns to the board. He again suggested that we stop meddling."

"He can't prevent us from addressing the board at a public meeting. I read about a case in Prince William County, Virginia, where the court ruled that the school board violated the First Amendment when it barred a principal from speaking. I suggest you call an emergency meeting of the MMMA soon—tonight if possible. We are going to have to come up with something dramatic to convince the school board to reconsider some of the contract proposals. Maybe we ought to consider a strike. Dr. Dillon and the board would not want to explain that to the public."

"It appears we must fight to maintain our role as members of management. Right now that role is being redefined for us by the board and teachers in negotiations. I don't know if they realize it, but the effect is wiping us out. Obviously, we cannot depend on Dr. Dillon or the board to protect our rights. Maybe a principals' strike would shake them up. I'll get as many principals as I can to meet here in my office tonight at 8:00 P.M.," said George.

"And I will make a call to my friend Clair Jones of the *Times*," replied Sidney.

THE MEDDLING MIDDLE MANAGERS

Questions for Discussion

1. What are the major issues in this case?
2. What are the major problems in the consolidation of school districts?
3. Why did the teachers get more attention and consideration than the principals did during the consolidation to form the Middleton County School District?
4. Why did the principals decide to form a bargaining unit?
5. Why was Superintendent Vincent Dillon so angry when he learned that the principals were organizing a bargaining unit?
6. Why did the Middleton teachers propose collective bargaining issues that would limit the power of the principals?
7. How would approval of the issues proposed by the teachers' association affect the principals' jobs?
8. What would you do about these problems if you were a Middleton School District principal? Why?

PART TWO

THE SCOPE AND DYNAMICS OF COLLECTIVE BARGAINING

Collective bargaining agendas are made up of demands and proposals. Understanding the use of the agenda is important in the negotiation process. When approved and adopted by both parties, the agenda gives direction to the negotiation process and allows time needed for advance preparation. Substantive agenda items calling for background information and considerable research should be scheduled as far in advance as possible. These items may have to be discussed and reconsidered at several meetings. If possible, issues most likely to be settled should be listed first on the agenda. A sense of accomplishment and agreement can thus be established early. Frequently, economic and noneconomic issues are separated for agenda purposes. Because the agenda is negotiable, parties unable to readily agree on a common agenda may want to try a rotating process. Then all they need to decide is who sets the first agenda item.

Discussions of agenda rules should include agreement on a procedure for proposing issues that just pop up—those that have not been included on the agenda. If the process of negotiation is to be evolutionary, unanticipated issues are bound to come up. Certain issues may develop naturally during bargaining. If the parties allow no flexibility and are stuck with a rigid, formal agenda procedure, issues that emerge naturally as part of an ongoing discussion are denied a hearing. Sometimes, one thing leads to another, which blends with another, which could, if discussed, contribute to a final agreement. If the parties are bound to a rigid agenda that allows no deviations, important and significant options for closure may be passed over.

The agenda is but one subject for the ground rules to be set before actual negotiations begin. Ground rules usually also include other issues, such as location of bargaining, rules of caucus, time and length of sessions, and possibly deadlines.

Case 6, "Who Needs an Agenda?" deals with several aspects of the ground rule and agenda issues. When ground rules and agenda bind the parties to a pattern that allows little flexibility, unanticipated issues are often held for ransom.

THE SCOPE OF BARGAINING

The scope of bargaining refers to the status of subjects that may or may not be negotiable. What's negotiable?

Just trying to determine what is and is not negotiable may stalemate the bargaining process. There are the mandatory issues that must be bargained, the nonmandatory ones that need not be bargained, and a host of issues and positions in between. For example, in some states the reduction of staff is not negotiable but the impact of that staff reduction is. In New York State, the distribution method for the Excellence in Teaching Award (bonus) must be negotiated separately from other contract negotiations. This award usually is not a part of the regular salary payment to teachers. Now cause exists for two impasse situations. When the parties are negotiating a successor contract and the awards distribution at the same time, which should be settled first?

In collective bargaining, the duty of the negotiating parties is to make a good-faith attempt to reach an agreement concerning wages, hours, and other terms and conditions of employment. Wages and hours need little interpretation. But what are other terms and conditions of employment?

What else is negotiable? The scope of subjects open to bargaining varies from state to state, and in some cases changes from one month to the next. Court and state agency decisions constantly affect the status of bargaining issues. What is nonmandatory today may be mandatory tomorrow. Courts must also settle differences when state laws are inconsistent and contradictory. For example, when agency fee becomes part of the negotiated contract, can a tenured teacher be fired for refusing to pay the agency fee?

The public sector borrowed freely from the private sector initially regarding only mandatory issues—wages, hours, and the generally recognized conditions of employment. But it did not stop there. Public employees, specifically teachers, were not satisfied with just those issues.

Teachers have consistently expanded the scope of bargaining to include class size, curriculum decisions, hiring standards, textbook selection, evaluation criteria and procedures, and staff development decisions, to name a few. That the scope of bargaining broadens as time passes appears inevitable.

Surveys indicate the following as the priority negotiation issues of school district employers and employees: salary, health and life insurance, length of school day, school calendar, class size, teacher assignments, performance evaluations, and work load.

Priority issues of county and municipal employers and employees include wages, benefits, clothing allowance, paid leaves, residency requirements, and work assignments.

Public school boards and municipal and county councils are becoming more aggressive in collective bargaining. The elected policy makers are taking the initiative by developing proposals that attempt to undo some of the problems created during previous negotiations. Management rights issues have high priority on management's list of bargaining proposals. Public employers are no longer willing to merely "hold the line" in answer to aggressive unions. They are seeking concessions in health benefits and are demanding other "rollbacks" when they can demonstrate the necessity for such action. Examples of concessions being realized by public employers are consideration of merit pay proposals, addition of a management rights clause, revision of rights to transfer teachers, additional restrictions on personal days, and employee contribution to health costs.

Public employees forcefully resist employers' "rollback" and "takeback" proposals. In Case 7, "Watercooler Diplomacy," the employees' association counters the district's rollback proposal to allow volunteer parents to drive buses with a retaliatory measure of their own. As the bargaining process deteriorates into a negotiation of positions rather than issues, impasse seems inevitable. When the local representatives on the negotiating team clash, the two professional negotiators meet at the watercooler.

BARGAINING DYNAMICS AND STYLE

One of the most difficult problems to overcome in bargaining is separating the people from the issues. Both parties sometimes come to the table with strong feelings about the personalities involved. The atmosphere at the negotiating table may change dramatically when new participants are brought into the process. Parties convinced that in-house, local negotiations have been successful, as a rule, resent the introduction of a hired professional negotiator during the process. This is especially true if the hired gun changes the climate of negotiations by using sarcasm and ridicule as bargaining techniques or if current and previous contracts are criticized. Denouncing the current contract as inadequate and inept also condemns those who negotiated it. Case 8, "The Hired Gun and His Donkey," illustrates what can happen when an immature and unprofessional "professional" uses questionable tactics at the table.

The temperament and demeanor of the negotiators at the table set the stage for the negotiation session. Initial meetings usually accomplish nothing more than an exchange of lists of issues to be negotiated. After that, the real working sessions begin. In the usual course of things, the less important items are negotiated first. This allows the parties to experience agreement and success before tackling the more troublesome issues.

How do you sustain a negotiation that is coming apart at the seams because of personality conflicts? How do you deal with a negotiator who refuses to negotiate? How do you handle an opponent who believes that he or she has a mandate from the people to regain control of the organization?

Upon encountering a hostile opponent, most negotiators would be inclined to (a) throw up their hands in despair, professing the futility of dealing with the fool, and walk out; or (b) back off, recognizing what is happening, accept the fact that the hostility is going to have to be dealt with, and adjust negotiation strategy accordingly. Obviously, the latter is the choice to make if a final agreement is the goal.

Probably no situation in the negotiation process requires more planning and preparation than bargaining with a hostile opponent. The first order of business is to determine what form the hostility is taking. Planning a counterbalancing strategy requires an awareness of and a focus on the kinds of behavior being used. Does the opponent use disruptive tactics? Is the problem an uncooperative attitude? Are sarcasm and ridicule used? Does the opponent make a practice of interrupting, show a lack of respect, or demonstrate a need to dominate? Look for clues about your opponent's attitude and style. Because most people tend to stick with a negotiating style they believe works for them, try to find information about your opponent's past negotiations.

As you analyze your opponent's behavior, consider the possibility that his or her conduct may be a ploy to control the situation and proceedings. Whatever your conclusion, you are going to have to contend with the problem if you want to continue the negotiations. That probably means that it will be up to you to change the climate of the proceedings by introducing an alternative, positive style. Tempers must be allowed to simmer down and emotions to return to normal. When you squelch hostile behavior by offering creative and supportive alternatives, you regain control of the path and direction the negotiations will take. Remember that for almost every issue or problem there are a number of alternative solutions and answers. People tend to zero in on one solution and don't really look for others. This limits creativity in solving problems.

When the bargaining climate has been changed from one of confrontation to one of cooperation, a successful conclusion to negotiations for both parties is possible. Case 9, "Dealing With the Hostile Opposer," demonstrates how one professional union negotiator found a lemon and made lemonade.

Experienced negotiators eventually develop a bargaining style that, in their minds, works for them. One negotiator classifies all bargaining proposals as economic or noneconomic issues. Another insists on settling all noneconomic issues before talking about the economic proposals. A third negotiator discusses economic issues only as a package that must be considered together. Some negotiators do not sign off on tentative agreements until all issues are resolved. Authorities agree that there are about as many bargaining styles as there are negotiators. The universally recognized "best" bargaining style probably does not exist.

Parties to negotiation get used to each other's style and, after a time, come to expect it. When the style is abruptly altered by a new spokesperson for one or the other of the parties, frustration and anger often result. This, in turn, may lead to excessive countermeasures by the other side, resulting in near-impasse situations. When substantive procedural changes are proposed, the sponsoring party must explain the rationale and consequence of such changes. Because most negotiations call for a series of trade-offs, both parties should support a bargaining style that allows flexibility and a creative use of alternatives.

Another form of negotiation takes place within the bargaining team and between it and the team's constituency. Agreements have to be reached there, too. It is important for the negotiating team to be prepared, organized, and of one mind regarding bargaining procedures. Only the chief negotiator speaks for the group. Team decisions are made in caucus and are articulated by the spokesperson. At least one member of the team is designated as official note taker. Notes are important to refresh memories and to serve as records of bargaining sessions. Usually they are the only records of the meetings. Case 10, "The Moment of Impasse," deals with some of the procedural bargaining problems. It illustrates how and why trade-offs are made during discussion sessions.

Generally recognized principles and guidelines for collective bargaining include, among others, the following:

(1) Agree on a set of ground rules at the beginning of negotiations. Ground rules should include, at least, the following: a schedule of meetings, rules on press releases, caucusing procedures, procedures for handling tentative agreements, and what constitutes a quorum.

(2) When bargaining, take into account the advantages of an improvement in long-term relationships versus the gain of a short-term concession.

(3) Never say never. You probably will regret it.

(4) Share relevant information with the other party.

(5) Develop an agenda for negotiation meetings, but allow a degree of flexibility.

(6) Negotiate issues and party interests, not fixed positions.

(7) Although you may take a final position on issues, avoid making proposals on a take-it-or-leave-it basis.

(8) Don't allow personalities to influence the bargaining process.

(9) Decide whether your negotiating team will allow its members to make side agreements.

(10) Use a joint study committee or side letter of agreement as a way of getting around sensitive and complicated issues that are holding up closure.

C A S E   S I X

WHO NEEDS AN AGENDA?

At 7:15 P.M., Harry Markel, superintendent of the Blairsburg Consolidated School District, tapped his water glass lightly to get the attention of those around the table. "Before we begin what we all anticipate will be our final negotiation session for a new contract, I would like to personally thank the members of both negotiation teams, especially the negotiators, for your efforts in the process this year. By the end of our meeting two weeks ago, we knew we were close to settlement. I don't want what I'm about to say to jeopardize that. With the permission of the federation, I would like to offer a new proposal that is not on the agenda for tonight."

"It's not on the agenda?" interrupted Erwin Addison, negotiator for the Blairsburg Service Staff Federation.

"That's right. If you will direct your attention to the copy of our proposal I'm distributing right now, I will explain..."

"Could I interrupt a minute, Harry?" said Erwin. "Why are you taking over? Are you now the negotiator for the school district?"

"No, I'm not," replied Harry, "and if you give me a chance, I'll explain the unusual circumstances that we think warrant consideration of the proposal we have here."

"Harry, I should not have to remind you, of all people, what Article 1.4 of the current contract says, and the reason you insisted that that specific language be added to the contract three years ago," said Erwin. Flipping to the pertinent section of the current contract, he continued, "In case you don't remember, let me read the language you drafted for that article, 'At or before the first meeting to open negotiations, the parties will simultaneously exchange proposals concerning all issues presented for negotiation....The agenda for each meeting will be established at the previous meeting, with neither party introducing new or additional proposals unless it is mutually agreed upon in advance.' The District insisted on this article three years ago when we proposed discussion of an issue not included in our initial package. Have we seen this proposal of yours before?"

"If you give me the chance to talk about our proposal, I will make clear how the circumstances are different," said the superintendent. "May I explain?"

Erwin glanced at Dale Lamont, president of the local federation, and Victor Phelps, member of the local federation negotiation team, for some sign. Receiving none, he nodded in Harry's direction. "We'll have to hear this."

"Last Thursday," began Harry, "the district school board appointed our district negotiator, Steve Birdsall, supervisor of all nonteaching personnel. His title will be Supervisor of Service Staff. As our business manager, he has been acting, unofficially, in that capacity anyhow. I'm sure that is not news to your members since most of them have been dealing with Steve right along. The board also adopted a revised job description for this position, which will appear in the new policy manual.

"The new proposal we are asking you to consider would plug Steve into the grievance procedure by revising current language. Nonteaching personnel would present their grievances in writing to the Supervisor of Service Staff rather than to the superintendent."

"The scuttlebutt has it that the board decided to hire a full-time principal to help supervise teachers," said Victor Phelps. "Is that true?"

"No," replied Harry. "The board considered hiring a full-time principal but decided against it for financial reasons. We will continue with our elementary music teacher, Mr. Scott, serving as a part-time elementary supervisor."

"Getting back to your proposal," said Erwin, "even if we were willing to suspend the rules as you're requesting, why should we entertain your proposal? You want to add another step in the grievance process, which by my quick calculation adds another fifteen days."

"Additional days were not a major concern during our last negotiations, when you proposed changing the time an employee had to file a grievance from thirty calendar days to thirty school days. That would have added days," prompted Harry.

"And you said no!" shot back Erwin.

"I'd like to change the subject a bit," said Harry. "Earlier you asked if I was taking over negotiation for the district. Perhaps now it is clear why I wanted to explain the board's action and rationale for proposing a contract revision at this late date. Steve continues as our negotiator and will take over now that we are ready to discuss the issues."

"Are we ready?" asked Erwin. "Two issues are on the agenda for tonight's meeting: first, the eligibility of part-time bus drivers and cafeteria workers for specific fringe benefits and, second, the proposed increase in longevity pay. The federation has prepared a response to the district's last proposal that should settle the contract. The federation will accept the district's limitation of fringe benefits if the district will approve our requested increase in longevity pay. If that is not agreeable, we both withdraw our proposals. In either case, we have a contract."

"We certainly will consider that offer," said Steve Birdsall. "But what about the grievance issue?"

"I think we should address only the agenda items and not complicate them with your late grievance proposal," said Erwin. "I can tell you this without a caucus of the team. We will not willingly agree to another fifteen days added to the grievance procedure. If there is a way around that, I will ask the team to discuss the offer."

"Having anticipated that the federation might object to additional days, we are willing to write in a clause wherein the board would have the option of hearing the grievance. If the board elected to waive its hearing, the number of days would not change."

"And if the board didn't waive the hearing, the grievance procedure would be fifteen days longer," said Erwin. "That really does not alleviate our objection to the substance of your proposal. Why should we agree to your late proposal? What do we gain by doing so? You request a suspension of the agenda rule that you so adamantly demanded during our last negotiations. Now your attitude seems to be, who needs an agenda? When it suits your purpose, you move to suspend the rules so that your proposal to add fifteen days to the grievance procedure may be put on the table. Why should we agree to that? What incentive do you offer? What is it worth to you? As far as we are concerned, two issues remain on the agenda for discussion tonight. We have made you a counteroffer. What is your response?"

WHO NEEDS AN AGENDA?

Questions for Discussion

1. What would you select as the most important factors in this case?
2. How would you have responded to Superintendent Markel's initial request to discuss an issue that was not on the agenda?
3. What are the advantages and disadvantages of an agenda?
4. What larger issues does this case pose for you?
5. Do you see any way the district can get the new issue on the table for discussion?
6. How would you respond to Erwin Addison's last set of questions?

WATER COOLER DIPLOMACY

Vera Reid closed the door as she left the school district superintendent's office and just stood there. She looked to see if Betty, the superintendent's secretary, was watching her. Vera didn't want anyone to see how upset she was. She didn't have to worry. Betty was flipping pages in her appointment book, attempting to find a date for yet another meeting for someone on the phone.

Vera waved a quick good-bye as she passed through the outer office into the hall. Her mouth felt dry, so she headed for the watercooler across the hall. As she sipped the ice-cold water, a replay of the brief, frustrating meeting she just had with the superintendent came to mind. Why is the district holding so firm to its untenable position on the volunteer driver issue, Vera wondered. On the other hand, our association's proposal on bus washing also is impractical. As president of the Mallard Transportation Association, Vera has tried to get both groups to reconsider the two absurd issues that have stalled negotiations for months. As a result of her meeting with Superintendent Dressler, Vera is more convinced than ever that her association will have to make the first conciliatory move if this impasse is ever going to be settled. She is not confident that she can swing that.

THE MALLARD TRANSPORTATION ASSOCIATION

The Mallard Transportation Association is one of four collective bargaining units recognized by the Mallard Central School District. The Mallard

Teachers Association represents the full-time teachers; the Mallard Principals Association represents all administrators except the superintendent; and the Mallard Support Staff Federation represents all nonteaching employees except transportation employees.

When the state mandated collective bargaining eighteen years ago, the transportation employees petitioned the district to organize a bargaining unit separate from the other support staff. They cited uniqueness in that two-thirds of the membership were part-time employees. The group currently includes twenty-two full-time employees, including bus mechanics, bus maintenance workers, and full-time drivers, and forty-three part-time drivers, who work twenty or more hours per week. The part-time employees receive prorated benefits. The district also maintains a pool of fifteen substitute drivers who are not eligible for association membership and who work fewer than 20 hours per week.

The Mallard Central School District is the largest in the county and has one senior high school, two junior high schools, and six elementary buildings. The school district serves a large rural area in addition to the City of Mallard. The population of the city is currently listed as 28,500. The major industries include an electronics assembly plant, one of the largest furniture factories in the country, a large soft-drink bottling works, and various small manufacturing businesses. In addition, Mallard serves as the major shopping center for a five-county area.

The first mandated collective bargaining encounters in the Mallard district eighteen years ago were devastating. At one point, three of the four contracts up for negotiation were not settled by Labor Day, when school was about to start. Two of those went to fact-finding and were not resolved until after Christmas. The school board threatened to contract the transportation of pupils and get out of the business, and the employees threatened a strike.

When the smoke cleared, representatives of the school board, administration, and the bargaining units sat down and decided what had to be done to avoid a replay of that unhappy experience. The school board hired a negotiator who earned the confidence and respect of management and employees alike. The employee units let it be known to those who negotiated for them that they were not interested in needless confrontation and adversarial relationships. Collective bargaining in the Mallard Central School District has been uneventful for the past dozen years or so. There were those who thought things were too quiet, too easy. Is negotiation really effective if there is no conflict, no encounter?

THE BAND FLARE-UP

The Mallard Central Marching Band has earned the reputation of being one of the best in the state. Over the past five years, the band won two state championships and first place in almost all of the parade competitions it has entered. The popular band director, Warren Dalrymple, decides which of the many invitations to perform will be accepted. He submits his recommendation to the administration for a final decision. Of late, high school faculty and some parents have complained about the band schedule and the amount of school time lost by band members. Other school patrons have criticized the apparent cost of the many band excursions.

When the Band Mothers Organization (BMO) learned that the school board had the band schedule on the agenda of its next meeting, a delegation attended. The president of the BMO requested permission to address the board. She reminded the board of the school band's public relations value to the school district and to the community. She announced that eight substitute bus drivers who are parents of band members volunteered to drive band trips without pay. Because this would reduce expenses, she concluded that there was no need to curtail the band trips. The board briefly discussed the pros and cons of the band program and adjourned that agenda item with a request that the administration screen the trips carefully.

When Vera Reid heard what transpired at the board meeting, she called a meeting of her association's negotiation committee. In a letter to the board over Vera's signature, the association reminded the board that the current contract requires that drivers be assigned activity bus trips based on seniority. In reply, the board president wrote that volunteers would be used only when the trip involved special recognition of students. Although this was never explained, it was generally assumed that volunteer bus drivers would be used on rare occasions.

THE INCIDENT

Several months later, the state governor invited the Mallard school band, as one of six bands in the state, to take part in a special parade in the state capital. Because this was to be a three-day, two-night excursion, Barbara Henley, the school business manager, solicited volunteer drivers. When the Mallard Transportation Association got wind of this, Vera informed Barbara that if volunteers were used, the association would file a grievance. Barbara said that the administration considered this occasion special recognition of Mallard students. The volunteers would save the district a considerable amount of money because regular drivers would receive pay for three days. Besides, the district received more than enough volunteers.

On March 10, a week before the first negotiation meeting for a successor contract, the Mallard Transportation Association filed a grievance.

THE NEGOTIATION

The district negotiation team consists of Monica Dressler, school superintendent; Barbara Henley, district business manager; Marlin Scharf, district board member; and John Brewer, attorney and chief negotiator for the district. The association team is led by Paul Goodrich, association negotiator from the regional office, and includes Vera Reid, president of the local, and George Eller, chief bus mechanic and member of the local.

Among the proposals in the district's package that were exchanged during the first negotiation session was one that would revise contract language to allow volunteer bus drivers on all special bus trips. The association's proposals for contract revision included an article to be added to the contract that would require all substitute drivers to clean and wash the buses they use. This is currently the responsibility of the bus maintenance crew.

As negotiations moved ahead, the volunteer driver and bus washing issues, along with salary, emerged as the troublesome issues. By the end of the fourth negotiation session, only those remained unresolved. The district's most recent salary offer was a raise of 4 percent each year of the two-year contract, with a larger percentage allocated to new drivers. The result would be less than 4 percent for senior employees, who are the majority and who are represented on the negotiation committee. The association demanded a 10 percent increment each year of the two-year contract and was adamantly opposed to discriminating percentages.

During the fifth negotiating session, both parties moved one percentage point: the association reduced its demand to 9 percent, and the district offered 5 percent. Both parties realized that a compromise on salary would be necessary for settlement. But neither party appeared willing to yield on other issues. A sixth meeting was scheduled to make one more pass at settlement before declaring impasse and requesting the assistance of a state-appointed mediator.

THE WATERCOOLER INCIDENT

The negotiation team members moved about the boardroom selecting coffee, tea, or a soft drink at the small service area. Monica Dressler moved to her place at the table, which was the unofficial signal that it was time to begin.

Association negotiator Paul Goodrich waited until everyone was seated before he spoke, "Since our last meeting, Vera met with representatives of both parties and asked each of them to consider withdrawing issues other than salary increment. Superintendent Dressler's answer was that the district would hold firm on its last position. Members of the association she talked to were just as uncompromising. Unless we are determined to declare impasse, we must find a middle ground."

"The district made the last offer," said the district negotiator, John Brewer. "Is the association ready to make a counterproposal?"

"Yes, we are," responded Paul. "Our last request was for a 9 percent salary increase. If the district agrees to that, the association will agree to the differentiated payment to new drivers, as requested by the district. Thus, senior members will get only 8 percent, and the additional 1 percent will be distributed among new drivers."

"That's not much of a compromise," noted John. "Anything else?"

"No, let's deal with that," responded Paul.

"What about the other issues?" interrupted Marlin Scharf, the board member.

"No change," said Paul.

"Obviously, we need to caucus," said John. Because the boardroom is the district's home base, the association members slowly got up to leave.

The association members barely had time to settle in the teachers' lounge that they used for meetings when they were called back to the boardroom.

"We have considered your offer but cannot accept it as is," said John. "Your willingness to allow the differentiated pay is a move in the right direction. We cannot go for 9 percent. However, if you will accept our proposal on volunteer drivers, we will save money on that score and be willing to offer you 7 percent each year.

How does that sound?"

"Not acceptable!" shot back Paul. "Your proposal will give our senior drivers only a 6 percent raise and at the same time reduce their income by eliminating some extra bus trips for them. We won the grievance on that issue and we are not going to give away that extra income for our senior drivers. Besides, your proposal now calls for volunteers for all extra bus trips when originally it was only for band trips. I can tell you that one is not going to fly!"

"Well then, unless you have a counterproposal, I guess we are at impasse. Why don't you take some time to think it over?" suggested John.

"You know, if you held some of your teachers and activity people in line, you wouldn't have so many extra bus trips and expenses," said Vera.

"That's really none of your business!" shouted Marlin Scharf. "I've had enough of this. I suggest we call it quits."

An irate John Brewer said, "We can't just call it quits, Marlin. Eventually, we must come up with a new contract. Look, I suggest we take a thirty-minute recess to reassess our positions and come back to the table for one last shot. Agreed?"

"Why not?" said Paul, who led his team from the room.

John followed Paul out into the hall and fell into step beside him. "Buy you a drink?"

"Boy, could I use one," Paul said. "Unfortunately we'll have to settle for water. C'mon, I'll buy," he said as they headed for the watercooler around the corner and down the hall.

"How many weeks have we been at this—eight? It seems like eighty," said John. He took a long drink of water and continued, "I don't think this should have to go to mediation. Just between you and me, our problem now is the board member, Marlin. He claims the board is against any more compromises, and I know that's not true. I don't know why Monica is letting him get away with it."

"I know you can't shut him up," said Paul, smiling. "We are not anxious for mediation either, but my people will not buy the volunteer driver issue. Get that off the table and we can move."

"If I can get them to withdraw that, what is your bottom line on salary?" John asked. "Oh, and you will have to withdraw your bus washing proposal," he added.

"If you can get the district to withdraw the volunteer driver issue, I think we can look at a compromise of 8 percent the first year and 7 percent the second year of the two-year contract. Also, the differentiated percentage will apply only the first year. That will give our senior employees 7 percent each year and a bit of a bonus the first year for new drivers. Should satisfy both groups. We will also withdraw our bus washing proposal."

John took another drink of water and walked down the hall and back. "Tell you what," he said, "if you can convince your group to let you make that proposal when we get back in there, do it. If I can get to Monica before we meet and convince her that this is the best we can do, we may have a deal."

"And if you can't convince her?" asked Paul.

"Then I will ask her to support me when I present my recommendation to the whole board of education. Having lost the grievance, they should be willing to give up on that issue."

"Let's go for it," said Paul as he shook John's hand.

WATER COOLER DIPLOMACY

Questions for Discussion

1. What basic issues are involved in this case?
2. Why did the Mallard school board agree to use volunteer drivers for school band trips?
3. Do you agree with those who questioned the effectiveness of negotiation in the Mallard Central School District because it progressed too smoothly?
4. Why were the parties unwilling to compromise on certain critical issues?

5. If you were to arbitrate the unresolved issues before the watercooler meeting, what would be your recommendations? Why?
6. Was the deal made at the watercooler by the two negotiators fair to each negotiating party?
7. Should negotiators make deals and discuss compromises away from the table? Why?

THE HIRED GUN AND HIS DONKEY

I don't think I'll ever forget that meeting! There was our association's professional negotiator, Carter Crowell, blowing up an inflatable three-foot donkey. I was flabbergasted! All I could do was stare in disbelief as he seated the rubber donkey in the chair next to him. That's why he asked for an empty chair.

The Mill Creek School District negotiator, Victoria White, had just finished presenting an overview of the district's proposals in the opening round of this year's negotiations. Carter Crowell turned to that ridiculous rubber donkey on the chair beside him and said, "Can you believe the district's proposal? They actually want to reduce the meager benefits these good people have worked so hard to get. I think management is trying to make an ass out of us—Don't you?"

Stunned silence. Victoria White paled.

Dr. Martin Oakland, superintendent of the Mill Creek School District, was the first to speak. "This is preposterous! We are not going to sit here and take part in this charade." He turned to face me. "When you are ready to seriously negotiate on a professional level, let us know. Until then, we stand adjourned."

With that, Dr. Martin, Mrs. White, and Robert Gilligan, president of the Mill Creek School Board, filed out of the room to the adjacent superintendent's office.

Carter smiled as he tugged on a plug to deflate the donkey. "What's with them? Your people can't take a joke, can they? I thought we needed a little levity before I presented our proposals."

I couldn't speak. I wouldn't have known what to say anyhow. Joe Hoffman, a member of our negotiating committee, found words. "I don't pretend to know why you did that. You embarrassed us, ridiculed Mrs. White, and probably set negotiations back ten years in this district. I'm leaving too."

Carter turned to me and said, "When can we schedule another meeting?"

"I have no idea, and I'm leaving too. I'll be in touch. You know, that was really dumb," was all I could say.

Several days later, the following memo was delivered to my office next door to the school cafeteria, which I manage.

TO: **Mrs. Beverly Keeler**
             President
             Mill Creek Support Staff Association

FROM: **Dr. Martin Oakland**
             Superintendent
             Mill Creek School District

SUBJECT: Professional Negotiation Conduct

The inexcusable behavior of your association's negotiator at our initial meeting last night causes us a great deal of concern. Until that unfortunate incident, we expected negotiations to run smoothly again this year.

At your request and in a spirit of cooperation, our negotiator, Mrs. Victoria White, agreed to present the district's set of proposals first. Mr. Crowell's unseemly and crude response to those proposals shocked all of us at the table.

Mrs. White demands that Crowell be fired and an apology be offered by your association. Mr. Gilligan and I suggest that, for the good of all concerned, Mr. Crowell withdraw from these negotiations. He made a mockery of the collective bargaining process. I am sure you and your association members will agree that his conduct warrants this drastic action. In fact, I know that Joe Hoffman, the other employee on your negotiation team, agrees with our suggestion.

Please let us know when your group is prepared to meet, and who will represent your association during negotiations.

I read the memo again before dialing the custodian's workroom number. I asked the person who answered to speak to Joe Hoffman. "Joe, when did you talk to Dr. Oakland about our meeting the other night?"

"Yesterday when I came to work he was waiting for me in the hall near our workroom. He asked me what I thought of the meeting and I told him it was a disgrace. I agreed with him that Crowell should be fired."

"You had no business talking to him about the meeting. I am the president and spokesperson for the association. You're going to have to get used to that."

"I was giving my personal opinion. Anyway, somebody from the association has to let them know we don't approve of Crowell's antics. You should have said something that night, but you didn't. You just let them walk out. By the way, how did you know I talked to Oakland?"

"I received a memo from Dr. Oakland suggesting that Crowell resign as negotiator and calling for an apology from the association. If you can break away now, let's get together. We must arrange a meeting of the negotiation advisory committee as soon as possible."

While waiting for Joe, I began to think about how I got us into this mess. I guess I should have kept out of it. At least we had harmony when Joe was negotiating for us.

Joe Hoffman is one of our building custodian supervisors and is serving his twentieth year as a member of the association's negotiation committee here in Mill Creek. As president of the local, Joe negotiated the association's first ten contracts. And he was good at it. He got along with just about everyone in the unit, and that's no small accomplishment. Our unit negotiates for all employees in the district except the professional staff. That takes in a wide variety of interests because our unit includes bus drivers, bus mechanics, custodians, cafeteria workers, clerical workers, nurses, and a grounds keeper. Each of these groups had its own agenda of critical and top-priority issues to negotiate. Joe was able to sift through the proposals and come up with a package that pleased just about everybody. You knew that if some of your priority proposals were not on Joe's list this year, they would probably be included next time.

Then, two years ago the association decided to affiliate with the state organization and request the services of a professional negotiator. We seemed to be falling further and further behind other school districts in economic benefits. I campaigned for the presidency and the vote for affiliation. We won by only two votes, and Joe was elected vice president.

Benjamin Toon, an association representative, negotiated the first contract under the new arrangement. He and Victoria White hit it off from the very first meeting. Although we didn't gain as much economically as we had hoped to with the new contract, most of us believed we were on the right track. Ben Toon explained that we could not hope to catch up to other districts in one year. We accepted that and looked forward to the next contract negotiation.

As contract time rolled around, I received a letter from the state association stating that Benjamin Toon resigned to take a job in the private sector. A Mr. Carter Crowell was hired to take over Ben's former districts. The letter went on to say that, although this is Mr. Crowell's first year as a full-time association representative, he negotiated for a number of local associations while teaching.

Our first meeting with Carter Crowell started off pleasant enough. He asked a lot of questions about the history of negotiations in our district and about the members of management's negotiating team. He seemed particularly interested in hearing all we could tell him about Victoria White, who was hired to negotiate for the district at the time Ben Toon appeared on the scene. Carter summarized his experience as a teacher and negotiator. I think all of us were surprised at the number of teaching jobs he had held in seven different school districts during the last eighteen years.

Carter distributed a ten-page draft of negotiation proposals labeled *A-1* through *A-31*. He suggested that these form the basis of the association's package of issues for the upcoming negotiations. He repeatedly stressed how much time he spent analyzing our previous contracts in relation to contracts of employees in area school districts. According to Carter, we were so far behind economically that we may never catch up. Listening to him was depressing.

I suggested that we needed time to study the issues before even discussing them. This agitated Crowell. "I have already spent a great deal of time analyzing your current and previous contracts. That is my job." He continued condescendingly, "In my humble opinion, you have one of the worst contracts I've seen. That is undoubtedly due to your ineffective local negotiations. Each year the district takes advantage of your amateur, home-grown process, causing you to fall further and further behind. You should not have tried to go it alone without professional advice. Now, do you or do you not want equal salaries, benefits, and working conditions?"

I glanced at Joe Hoffman to get his reaction to this outburst. I didn't have to wait. Joe stood up and walked toward the door. "I'm leaving," he said. "There is no point in discussing the items on this list until we have had a chance to study them. Mr. Crowell, we will let you know when we are ready for another meeting. I see no point in continuing this discussion." With that, Joe left.

I told Crowell that I, too, was upset by his remarks because they represented a direct criticism of Joe and the way he had conducted previous negotiations. Crowell merely confirmed that that was what he intended. He said he expected to be invited to our meeting at which the issues would be discussed, and he left.

That first meeting with Crowell should have given us a clue of what we might be in for. And it would have, except our second meeting with him proved productive and came off without serious confrontation. The scope of issues on Carter's list impressed the other four members of our local negotiation advisory committee. An open-minded, candid discussion of the issues resulted in the selection of twenty-one of Carter's suggestions as our final negotiation package. Carter expressed disappointment that ten items did not survive the cut. Joe insisted that we were asking for too much too soon. But, by and large, we felt ready for the initial negotiation session scheduled for the following week. At least, we thought we were. And now we had this problem, and I felt responsible.

I opened the next meeting of the negotiation advisory committee with a review of what happened at the first negotiation session. As I described the antics of our negotiator, our members sat in stunned silence. While distributing a copy of the memo from Superintendent Oakland, I asked Joe if there was anything he wanted to add.

"I would like to point out that during two of the three meetings with Carter Crowell, he became so abrasive and obnoxious that people were compelled to walk out," Joe said. "He cannot continue as our negotiator. Either the state association assigns someone else or we must do something. As you remember, I was not in favor of affiliation to begin with. Maybe we should reconsider that decision by putting the issue up for another vote of the membership."

"I know you are still feeling bruised by your loss in the last election," I said, "but that is not the issue now. Our members voted for affiliation because our salaries and benefits don't come up to the average of other districts. The question before us is not whether we disaffiliate but how we get negotiations back on track."

"I don't think we can give in to the district on this," replied a bus drivers' representative. "No reflection on you, Joe, but a lot of us think we should have a professional negotiator in there. An outsider doesn't have to worry about personal relationships. He can go for the jugular, if that's what it takes."

"My God! Is that what we've come to?" asked Joe. "If so, Carter Crowell is your man."

"I side with Joe on this," said another custodians' representative, "even though I voted for affiliation. I think all of us were pleased with the way Ben Toon negotiated two years ago. The problem is not affiliation or the state association. The problem is Carter Crowell, and I think he should go. We must say that to the state association."

"We don't need strained relations with the district at this time," said another committee member.

"And we don't want to antagonize our state association."

As discussion continued, I saw that two committee members supported Joe's contention that under no circumstances should Carter Crowell be allowed to continue negotiating for the association. The other two committee members did not want to give in to the district's demands cited in the memorandum. With the discussion degenerating into heated and repetitious arguments that were getting nowhere, I rapped the table with a book to regain order.

"I think I know how each of you feels about the situation. As a committee, we seem to be pretty evenly divided. That doesn't help. I must confess I didn't bargain for this when I ran for the presidency of the association. I also admit that I don't have a strong sense of what to do in this case. We must compromise. Keep in mind the superintendent's memorandum. How should I respond to that memo? What do you see as our options?"

THE HIRED GUN AND HIS DONKEY

Questions for Discussion

1. What issues are involved in this case?
2. What factors persuaded the support staff members to affiliate with the parent state association?
3. Do you agree with the district's decision to suspend further discussion and the conditions laid down to renew negotiations? Why?
4. What is your reaction to Carter Crowell's ten page list of thirty-one issues that the association was to adopt as its package of proposals for negotiation with the District?
5. What factors worked to introduce a period of tension between the local association and the State Association in this case?
6. How would you answer Beverly Keeler's last question?

CASE NINE

DEALING WITH THE HOSTILE OPPOSER

Monty Parker, president of the Harlan Teachers Association, slammed his legal pad down on the table, threw his pen halfway across it, and tipped his chair back, balancing on the back two legs. Glaring at district negotiator Robert Coleman on the opposite side of the table and trying to control his voice, he said, "I don't know how to deal with a management negotiator who refuses to negotiate. We really didn't have this kind of problem until you started negotiating for the school district. We had some of the same problems two years ago. You demanded that we immediately drop a number of our proposals, and you refused to sign off on any issues until all issues were settled. Do you really think those tactics facilitate settlement?"

Ignoring the question, an enraged Coleman responded, "Mr. Parker, we have not refused to negotiate. We do refuse to take seriously the union's laundry list of outrageous proposals. That was made clear to you at our first meeting two weeks ago. You say you don't know how to deal with us?

Well, we don't know how to deal with your package of twenty-eight proposals, most of which call for unwarranted increased expenditures. Your package contains almost every 'buzz' issue I've heard of this year. We thought you would come to your senses, take our advice, and present a more reasonable set of demands tonight. I don't see..."

"Excuse me," interrupted Sam Kirkland, the association's negotiator. "The Harlan teachers' negotiating committee met and reaffirmed its support of its initial proposal. Tonight we came prepared to negotiate—did you?"

"Unless you reduce your demands, we really have nothing to say," replied Coleman. Tossing the association's thirty-page stapled set of proposals across the table, he continued, "Why don't you take this bulky, ill-advised document back and cut it by 50 percent. Then we can begin serious discussion of realistic and manageable proposals."

"Not on your life!" shouted Kirkland. "The ball is in your court, Coleman. You have our set of proposals," he said as he pushed the association document back across the table. "If you want to tell us which of those proposals are acceptable, or unacceptable, we can begin negotiating."

"I see no point in continuing this bickering," said Coleman as he pushed his chair back and stood up. "For a long time the association has pretty much had its way here in Harlan. The message the board is getting is that the public wants to see the board in control. The union is no longer going to get everything it asks for."

"How would you know what the public in this community wants?" responded Monty Parker. Looking directly at Bernard Perkins, the school board representative on the committee, Parker continued, "I live in this community and I can't believe that the public, much less the school board, wants to encourage an adversarial relationship between the teachers and the administration. I doubt you'd be talking like this if Superintendent Barger were here. Is he coming tonight?"

Bernard Perkins spoke for the first time. "Harold had another appointment but said he would be here. Can we hold off any further discussion until he comes?"

"It doesn't appear we'll be here much longer," said Monty Parker. "What do you think, Sam?"

Kirkland glanced in the direction of Jim Elliott and Lois Proctor, the other two teachers on the negotiation team. "I repeat, we are willing to negotiate. We are waiting for the district to respond to our last package offer. I would remind the district's negotiator that refusing to negotiate is an improper practice. Labor law in this state requires negotiators to come to the table with an open mind and with intent to reach agreement. Negotiators must be willing to discuss issues and explain reasons for taking certain positions. Negotiators are to consider alternatives. You, Mr. Coleman, have refused to do anything except exchange initial proposals."

Unmoved by Kirkland's interpretation of the law, Coleman turned to leave the room and said, "I'll notify the State Public Relations Board that we're at impasse."

As Bernard Perkins rose from his chair to follow Coleman out of the room, Kirkland asked, "Is this what the board really wants? Why are you board members sitting by and allowing Coleman to take us to impasse?" Perkins hesitated at the door, turned toward the association's team and replied, "No, I'm sure we don't want this. I'll talk to the board and Superintendent Barger."

When the district's team had left the room, Monty Parker shrugged his shoulders, raising his arms palms up, and addressed no one in particular, "How in the hell do you negotiate with arrogant hostility like that?"

HARLAN SCHOOL DISTRICT

With the advent of collective bargaining for all state public employees, the Harlan school board approved applications from two groups of employees for bargaining unit recognition: the Harlan Teachers Association and the Support Service Federation. Public sector bargaining during those first years often ended up as a do-it-yourself operation. The unions could not provide enough bargaining representatives to help the locals, and the public employers could not find "hired guns" to negotiate for management. Thus, Harlan, like many school districts, decided to negotiate "in-house" rather than wait in line for help. The state associations conducted weekend workshops for teachers and other employees who would be negotiating. The State School Board Association and administrators' organizations addressed the subject in state and regional meetings and provided negotiation guidelines in their journals and brochures.

In one sense, Superintendent Barger at least shared the blame for the fact that Harlan was now heading into its first bargaining impasse. During his interview for the superintendency, Barger made it clear that he was not in favor of "in-house" bargaining. He favored using professional negotiators. "In the first place," he said, "professional negotiators know what they are doing and how to do it. But more importantly, professionals take the heat when there is more heat than light; and when the smoke clears, they have left town. There is less danger of creating a strong adversarial relationship between employer and employees." Barger also pointed out the disadvantages of using professionals, not the least of which is the cost. He also cautioned that professionals sometimes create "issues" that have not been problems in the district.

The Harlan board accepted its new superintendent's recommendation and hired a lawyer from a neighboring village as district negotiator. The two Harlan employee groups subsequently requested negotiators from their state organizations. The board was pleased that several two-year contracts were negotiated without serious incident.

Then Robert Coleman was hired. He was selected by the board to replace the district's first hired negotiator, who retired. Robert Coleman impressed the board with his ideas of how management could both save money and reassure the public that control of the schools had not been surrendered to the unions. Barger suspected that Coleman's glib panaceas were more than coincidence. Coleman obviously had seen the editorials and letters to the editor in the local newspaper criticizing the school board for the annual tax increases needed to finance generous union agreements. Other remarks made by Coleman during the interview contributed to the uneasy feeling Barger had about the man. He would come to regret that he had not warned the board of his reservations.

The new negotiator patiently led the district's negotiating committee in an evaluation of the current contracts, suggesting a dozen or more substitutions of contract language. When Barger warned that some of the suggested language changes would roll back current benefits and thus prove unacceptable to the union, Coleman backed off. However, the implied cost savings were not lost on the board. Coleman convinced the board that it was to its advantage to wait until all issues were settled before signing off on any of them. This negotiating gambit almost resulted in an impasse during Coleman's first negotiation with the support staff. A dispirited union reluctantly accepted the district's last offer and signed a contract in late November. Coleman had pressed the point by warning that retroactivity could become an issue if the contract were not signed by Thanksgiving.

Employee criticism of Coleman's bargaining tactics moved the school board to reconsider using him as negotiator during the next round of bargaining. Ultimately, the board did not accept Superintendent Barger's recommendation and again hired Coleman.

THE MEDIATOR

The state-appointed mediator, Debra Babcock, tapped on the table while calling the meeting to order. "I asked both negotiation teams to this meeting so all parties concerned could hear the decision I have made in this case. The information our office received with your declaration of impasse did not tell the whole story here—it was incomplete, to say the least. According to information I now have, you have held only two meetings, at which nothing was resolved. Your declaration of impasse is premature. You have not really tried negotiation.

"This afternoon I met with Mr. Coleman and Mr. Kirkland. I suggested that the parties again start negotiating, and they agreed. As long as you're here tonight, you might just as well start now. You have exchanged your initial packages, so you start with that. Before you leave here tonight, set regular negotiation dates and times. You will find it helpful to set an agenda for each subsequent meeting. Any questions?"

"We thought you would be conducting a mediation session tonight, so our team will need to caucus," said Kirkland.

"Of course," said Debra Babcock, "and I assume the district could also use some time. Right?" she asked, looking at Coleman.

"Yes," responded Coleman. "The association should take all the time it needs to reduce the number of proposals."

Ignoring the zinger, Babcock said, "I'm going to leave you to your negotiations. I suggest you caucus for about an hour and meet back here to begin serious negotiations. I informed the negotiators that I am willing to come back, if necessary, after you have seriously attempted to negotiate. Good luck!" With that, Debra Babcock picked up her briefcase and headed for the door.

"We'll see you back here in about an hour," said Kirkland as Monty Parker led the employees' team from the room.

THE CAUCUS

The faculty used their lounge on the first floor as home base during negotiations. As the team members filed into the room, they helped themselves to the coffee and soft drinks on hand. Monty Parker took a sip of Diet Coke, sat down in one of the beat-up chairs, and turned toward the team's negotiator. "Sam, I hope you know what to do now, because I sure as hell don't."

"Since our last meeting, I've had time to cool off and think about our next move," replied Kirkland. "Debra Babcock suggested a couple of tactics when we met this afternoon. From what she's heard, Coleman takes pride in acting the hostile opponent. We saw some of that during negotiations for our last contract. For example, we know that he will not sign off on issues as they're settled. We know that he will want to package the issues in at least two major categories: economic and noneconomic. And," continued Kirkland, smiling, "we know that his insufferable personality will eventually get in the way of a settlement.

"I've come to the conclusion that Coleman's bargaining behavior is a style he uses as a means of control. Whatever the reason for his hostility, we are going to have to deal with Coleman to get a contract. We can't just throw up our hands and walk away, rationalizing that it is impossible to do business with him. So, the question becomes not whether we will negotiate with Coleman, but rather how we negotiate with him. Any ideas?"

The four members of the teachers' negotiating team glanced from one to the other. Jim Elliott said, "Two elements set Coleman off at our first meeting. One was the number of issues in our package, and the other was his estimate of the cost of our economic issues. Coleman insisted that we reduce the number of issues. Must we do that to get negotiations started again?"

"We are not going to do that," responded Kirkland emphatically. "Nor are we going to allow them to summarily reject all issues because they consider them too costly, or ludicrous, or whatever. We will expect management to respond categorically and responsibly to each of our issues, as we will to theirs.

"Now, in order to accomplish this we must change the negative climate that has prevailed during these negotiations. By changing the spirit and mood from one of confrontation to a more moderate atmosphere in which ideas can be exchanged and discussed, we stand a better chance of reviving the negotiation process. In order to get these negotiations back on track, we will counter hostile behavior with a positive, supportive posture. If Coleman continues to act obstinate and arbitrary, we will offer more creative alternatives; if he turns defensive, we will be understanding. Any questions?"

"Aren't we going to come across as weak and wimpy?" asked Elliott.

"On the contrary," replied Kirkland, "we are going to control the direction that negotiation will take. Now, this is how we're going to begin...."

DEALING WITH THE HOSTILE OPPOSER

Questions for Discussion

1. What would you select as the important factors in this case?
2. In your opinion, was the declared impasse inevitable? Why?
3. What do you think of the way Debra Babcock, the mediator, handled the situation?
4. What factors in this case permitted Robert Coleman to dominate the district's position and strategy?
5. Do you think Sam Kirkland's revised bargaining strategy discussed during the caucus will result in win-win negotiations? Why?
6. If you were Sam Kirkland, how would you proceed to open the next negotiation session? Why?

THE MOMENT OF IMPASSE

Angela Boyle, president of the North West Independent School District Board of Education, slowly walked across the school parking lot toward her car. She inserted the key into the door lock of the new Crown Victoria but did not turn it. Instead, she turned to glance back at the school building she had just left. Should she go back and have it out with Frank Webb now or wait until things settled down a bit? Before she could decide, she was startled by another car that seemed to just appear in the next parking space. It was Chris Winkler, her fellow board member.

"Anything the matter, Angie?" he asked. "Lock yourself out again?" Angela was saddled with an undeserved notoriety for locking herself out of her car. At a recent school board meeting, she locked the car with the motor running. Her husband had to come twenty miles to unlock the car. And that happened only once.

"No, Chris," she answered, smiling, "I'm debating with myself whether to go back in there and talk to Frank."

"I wouldn't," Chris said. "Wait until we can talk to him together. If I could stay tonight, we could get it over with. But, as you know, I'm late now for a long-standing appointment with an important client." As Chris started to back out of the parking space, he said, "Wait."

Angela nodded. "I will. I'll call you tomorrow." She unlocked the car and seated herself behind the wheel, fastening the seat belt. Angela passed the school building while driving out of the parking lot. She noticed that the light was still on in the school superintendent's office. "Mr. Webb," she said, talking to herself, "how do we tell you that you're fired as district negotiator? No matter how we put it, the point is you no longer represent the district in the bargaining with teachers. You blew it. Why couldn't you see what was happening?"

BACKGROUND OF NEGOTIATIONS AT NORTH WEST

North West Independent School District was created when the State Education Department called for a reorganization of small central school districts. Three former central school districts, each with K–12 enrollments of 400 to 800 students, merged to form the North West district. North West Senior High School, Wilfred Junior High School, and the Appleton Elementary School were located in the village of Appleton, the largest of the three former central districts. Each of the two smaller villages in the new district—Clarion and Borland—maintains a K–6 elementary school.

The issue of collective bargaining almost scuttled initial discussions of consolidation. Two school districts used the same local attorney, who negotiated with a state-association-appointed representative. At Clarion, the superintendent negotiated for the district with local staff representatives of the two unions. Two of the central school districts' employee groups were affiliated with one state association; Appleton's with the other. The issue of employee representation was settled by elections supervised by the state board. The reorganized district school board agreed on a negotiator to represent the district during the first negotiations with the restructured employees' unions.

Several years after the consolidation, the president of the teachers' association approached the superintendent of the reorganized district with the suggestion that the two of them negotiate the next contract. The success of that venture encouraged the other two employees' unions to request local bargaining. During the next dozen years or so, the North West Independent School District was the envy of the area schools for the apparent ease with which it negotiated successor agreements. Then the superintendent announced his impending retirement.

One of the applicants for the superintendent's position was the high school principal of a relatively large school district in the central part of the state. Frank Webb impressed the board with his self-assurance and his articulated vision of the future for the North West Independent School District. One of the district's attractions for him, he said, was its history of tranquil labor relations. Shortly after Frank Webb was hired, he announced to the employees' associations that he would continue to represent the district at the bargaining table.

THE FIRST INCIDENT

The teachers' contract was the first to be renegotiated. At the first negotiation session, the association proposed, as a ground rule, that tentative agreements be reduced to writing and initialed by each side.

Frank Webb objected. "I don't think that's a good idea. We will want to see the whole package before we start writing off."

"But that's the way we've always done it. If we agree on something, why not get it off the table so we don't have to come back to it?" asked John Chandler, president of the association and negotiator.

"That's not the way I negotiate," replied Webb. "We can have a tentative agreement without signing off. I prefer to have agreements tentative pending a final settlement."

"Under those conditions, nothing is really off the table until the last item is agreed to," said Chandler with a sneer. "What if we can't agree on one or two proposals? Does that mean nothing is settled—that we're back to square one?"

"That's right," replied Webb. "My experience has been that this kind of arrangement puts pressure on both sides to reach that final agreement." Webb glanced at each member of the association's team across the table, grateful that no one challenged his claim of experience.

"We can't accept your argument and ask that you reconsider your position on that ground rule," said Chandler. "You can respond to our request at the next meeting. Since we agree on the other ground rules, I suggest we exchange proposals, clarify issues that need clarification, and adjourn. Each of us will need time to study the other's proposals. In the meantime, you should read a newsletter put out by the State School Board Association way back in 1968, when it found it necessary to warn its members, to quote, 'Reduce your agreements to writing promptly!'"

At the next negotiation session, Chandler and his two fellow teachers on the negotiation committee—Sue Anderson and Nathan Moore—were the first arrivals. As discussion got under way, Frank Webb waited for the write-off issue to come up. When it didn't, he assumed that the association had accepted his position. Approximately an hour into the meeting, Chris Winkler interrupted the proceedings, "Excuse me, but is that a tape recorder running in front of you, John?" All at the table looked in the direction his finger pointed. He was pointing to a pocket-size tape recorder, which had just clicked to rewind.

"How long has that been there running?" demanded Webb.

"Since the beginning of the meeting," replied Chandler.

"That's illegal!" shouted Webb. "You can't tape-record these meetings without our knowledge. We didn't even know you were recording."

"We feel we must have a record of our tentative agreements," said Chandler. "If you won't sign off, then we are going to record these sessions.

We are not going to go through months of bargaining and end up with nothing settled. Have you reconsidered writing off tentative agreements?"

Webb looked to Angela Boyle for a signal. Receiving none, he asked for a caucus. After Greg Becker, the district's business manager, had closed the door to the superintendent's office, Boyle turned to face Webb. "What's going on in there? I thought we agreed to their request to initial tentative agreements. Why didn't you tell them that?"

"When they didn't bring it up, I thought they had forgotten about it. I still think..."

"John Chandler has years of negotiating experience," Boyle said, interrupting him. "If you knew him, you would have realized that he is not going to pass over that kind of issue." Boyle glanced at Chris Winkler and continued, "That's the way we negotiated for years, and it worked. Now, let's go back in there and settle this problem once and for all. The purpose of this exercise, after all, is to arrive at a final agreement."

THE FINAL INCIDENT

By the end of seven long bargaining sessions over a period of three months, twenty-six of the twenty-nine original issues on the table had been initialed by both parties. Neither the board members nor the teachers at the table were happy with the conduct of negotiations. The animosity and adversarial relationship that had developed between the two negotiators prolonged the meetings, which usually ended on a sour note. Everyone would breathe a sigh of relief when the ordeal was over.

The three unresolved issues were salary, agency fee, and faculty meetings. Concerning the matter of salary, the teachers were asking for a 10 percent salary increase each year of the proposed two-year contract. The district's last offer was 6 percent each year.

Agency fee was a high-priority issue for the association. The relatively tranquil relationship between district management and employees over the years had worked to the disadvantage of the association. Some of the senior faculty members had dropped out, and an increasing number of new teachers were refusing to join. The district board had taken a firm stand against agency fee over the years.

The faculty meeting proposal was new. The North West district's first contract included the following language: "There may be one (1) building faculty meeting per month and one (1) district faculty meeting per month. Meetings may be more often, if absolutely necessary. Meetings will end no later than 4:30 P.M." The association proposed that the above language be replaced by the following: "After-school faculty meetings later than 3:30 P.M. shall not exceed one (1) per month and shall be compensated at the summer-school instructional rate." The association argued that other school districts have this kind of language and that teachers, especially the younger teachers, feel they should be compensated for professional meetings.

The eighth negotiation session opened with the district's presenting a counterproposal to the proposal submitted by the association at the previous meeting. The district offered a 7 percent salary increase the first year and 8 percent the second year, provided that the association withdraw its remaining two proposals.

"Your salary offer is certainly closer to an acceptable level," said John Chandler. "However, it isn't high enough to buy the other two proposals.'

"Do you mean to imply that the agency fee and faculty meeting proposals are for sale?" asked Webb. "If we bid high enough, they may be dropped?"

"I didn't say that," answered Chandler. "You're asking us to drop two of our top-priority items without a salary offer that we think is fair. If you really want to find out whether the two nonsalary issues are being held for ransom, why don't you offer us 10 percent salary increases?"

"Would that do it?" asked Webb.

"Are you making a proposal?"

"No, and we are not going to continue playing games with you," said Webb angrily. "We will never agree to a 20 percent salary increase over two years, and besides..."

Chandler interrupted, "We're really not interested in what you are never going to do. We would like to get this contract settled. To that end, we offer the following counterproposal: salary increments of 9 percent each year and approval of agency fee. We will withdraw our faculty meeting proposal with the condition that a committee made up of two administrative and two teacher representatives study the problem and develop recommendations by the end of this school year."

"We will never agree to that. You haven't really made concessions. My problem with current contract language regarding faculty meetings is that it is too restrictive. I can't imagine what a committee could come up with that I could agree to unless it recommends to eliminate all references to faculty meetings."

"There you go with that 'never' again," said Chandler, smiling.

"A problem during these negotiations from day one has been your insistence that bargaining revolve around positions. You confuse positions and interests. You have taken an inflexible position on the faculty meeting issue and, in a sense, for you it is nonnegotiable. Some of our teachers have complained about the number of after-school meetings called by one of the elementary principals that would not qualify under the 'absolutely necessary' clause of the contract. We happen to think that one way to limit unnecessary meetings is to require that teachers be paid for their professional services at a professional rate. On the other hand, we have offered to withdraw that proposal and have a study committee look into the problem and report back to us. We think that's a concession."

Before Webb could say anything, Boyle broke in, "Why don't we caucus?" Looking at Chandler, she pushed her chair back from the table. "Give us a few minutes," she said as she headed for the superintendent's office next door.

Thirty minutes later, the district's team returned to their places at the table. Frank Webb cleared his throat and began, "The district has a counteroffer that we think you will find acceptable. We agree to 9 percent each year of the two-year contract provided that you drop agency fee. We have teachers who have strong feelings about joining the association and we do not want to force them to join. If this continues to be a problem for you, we can address it at another time and perhaps in another way. The district agrees to the appointment of a committee to study the faculty meeting issue with the condition that the committee be composed of three administrators and two teachers. If these conditions are accep—"

"They are not!" shouted Chandler. "Why must you stack the committee? Is it because you have no intention of allowing an objective report? I've had it. We might just as well go home. We were very close to a settlement and probably would have one if you could leave well enough alone." Chandler glanced at each of his colleagues to see if they wanted to add anything, but they were already standing, ready to leave.

Angela Boyle also stood up. "Before we break up, I'd suggest we set another meeting date. John, I agree—we may be close to agreement. Chris Winkler is already late for a business appointment, so it is just as well we quit for tonight. Can we get together a week from tonight?"

John Chandler consulted briefly with his fellow teachers and replied, "We can meet at 8:30. Nat has a late coaching practice."

When the teachers were gone, Angela Boyle turned to Frank Webb and, attempting to control the anger in her voice, said, "Why did you do that? In our caucus we agreed to a 9 percent salary increase and to their committee proposal if they would drop agency fee. Why did you change the makeup of the committee by adding another administrator?"

"Because I cannot accept the possibility of acceptance of the association's position on this issue. I don't think the contract should limit the number of faculty meetings, nor should the district pay teachers for attending meetings. I could never accept that!"

Chris Winkler interrupted, "Angela, I really must leave. It appears we must get our act together before our meeting with the teachers next week. Call me."

Boyle began gathering her things together. "I'll call you tomorrow, Frank, to arrange a meeting of our group. In the meantime, I want to talk to other members of the board."

THE MOMENT OF IMPASSE

Questions for Discussion

1. How do you feel about Frank Webb's negotiation strategy of not signing off on issues? Why?
2. How does Frank Webb's demeanor during the first negotiation session impress you? Why?
3. Why do you think the teachers' association wanted to change the faculty meeting policy?
4. What were the contributing factors in the deterioration of professional and personal relations in this case?
5. How did Frank Webb's determination to negotiate position rather than issues affect these negotiations?
6. If you were a North West district board member, what would you do about Frank Webb?
7. How does this case illustrate the use of trade-offs in collective bargaining?
8. What other issues does this case pose for you? Why?

PART THREE

THE INFLUENCE OF PRESSURE IN BARGAINING

Pressures and pressure groups effectively influence collective bargaining. External sources can exert unwelcome pressures on all parties involved in negotiations. This is particularly true in the public sector, where a "third force"—the public—assumes a role. Private sector bargaining units may realize pressures from a board of directors, contract settlements in other companies, or competition for comparable settlements within the company. However, the private sector does not answer to the public in the same way that public sector organizations do.

The effects of pressures are more keenly felt in the public sector because negotiation is usually conducted by local units in relatively small settings: school districts, villages, and townships. This provincialism is further complicated by the fact that no one "public" represents all of the factions in the community. Various publics press their special interests on one or both negotiating parties. The village, county, town, and school boards, as well as the unions, have a host of constituencies vying for attention and power. The tax-conscious group demands that costs be kept down with no increase in taxes. The Chamber of Commerce requests more services and free parking for customers, which, if granted, might necessitate higher taxes. The PTA wants more teachers in order to reduce class size in the elementary schools. And the parents want more buses and shorter routes.

The negotiating parties in the public sector attempt to respond to the various local pressures in ways that will win public support for their positions on issues. The negotiating party that believes it has public support for its stand on a priority issue tends to hold that position optimistically, no matter how preposterous the proposal. And if negotiations drag on to the stage of impasse, the parties aggressively step up their campaigns for public consensus and support.

This can lead to bitter and prolonged "public" negotiations that aggravate an already bad situation.

Parents and other community citizens are becoming increasingly concerned about what they perceive to be happening at the bargaining table in their local school district and in their other community organizations. They see the current bargaining process as prohibiting them from learning what is happening at the bargaining table until the contract is signed and decisions are irreversible. If they disapprove of the final settlement, the public demands to know why information was not provided earlier.

The public is confused by and upset about the "them-and-us" syndrome perceived to exist between management and employees. How is this affecting children and the operation and management of the schools? Do the recently negotiated contracts really create conditions that prohibit supervisors from calling employees to work during an emergency? If negotiation becomes intense and hostile, especially when a strike is threatened, each party appeals to the public for support of its cause. And each side has its constituencies. The result is that, in some cases, the public demands drastic measures in exchange for its support. Even if not invited, the public now tends to get involved when its schools and its community services are threatened.

When two or more public employer organizations in the same community call on the same labor market for employees with similar skills and training, each employer feels the pressure to maintain salaries, benefits, and working conditions at about the same levels as those offered by the other employer. At the same time, the public manager is expected to satisfy the public's demands for fiscal responsibility and no tax increases. Case 11, "The Mayor Said...," illustrates the pressures and problems that occur when a city mayor is unable to offer city workers raises equal to those being offered to comparable school district workers. Other cases in this casebook, such as Case 18, "Fire the Teachers; Keep the Substitutes," present situations in which public pressure causes problems.

The repercussions of the excellence-in-education reform movement, launched in 1983 with the report *A Nation at Risk: The Imperative of School Reform*, exemplify another form of external pressure. Commissioned by the then Secretary of Education, Dr. Terrel Bell, the report charged that "the educational foundations of our society are presently eroded by a rising tide of mediocrity." In addition, the report indicated that the major responsibility of the federal government is to do just what the report claims to do: identify the national interest. The authors of the report proclaimed that the responsibility for educational reform belonged to the individual states.

The states responded by creating hundreds of reform proposals, including increased graduation requirements, merit pay schemes, career ladders, and increased certification standards. The result has been a hodgepodge of legislated and mandated programs, many of which affect public sector bargaining. For example, one state sought to promote teaching excellence by funding Excellence in Teaching (EIT) awards. On the whole, this was a worthy goal. However, the legislation creating the awards stipulated that the method of distributing the EIT grants to the teachers not only must be negotiated, but also must be negotiated separately from regular contract bargaining. Little, if any, thought was given to whether this award was a bonus or a part of the traditional salary schedule. Not only is the purpose of the EIT award not being realized in most cases, but the method of distribution has also complicated the negotiation process. Case 12, "Caught in the Middle," illustrates the problems and pressures that well-intentioned but ill-planned legislation can cause in bargaining. For all their reform efforts, state governments have not significantly improved the overall quality of education.

Internal pressures that also affect the negotiation process may evolve from within the bargaining units before, during, or after negotiations. School board members sometimes disagree with one another or with the chief school officer regarding issues and events in negotiation. County governments, with their weak management structure and their lack of a single executive authority, typically permit and encourage fragmentation of county workers for bargaining purposes. Parity and comparability pressures are inevitable when departments become "community-of-interest" bargaining units. Department bargaining units are forced to compete with one another for scarce resources and bargaining power. Some county legislatures, recognizing the discord that this kind of fragmentation causes, have restructured county government so that unionization occurs across department lines. That allows the development of a single personnel policy for all county employees. Bargaining problems related to the decentralized world of county government are addressed in Case 13, "But What About...?" The problems in this case would be relevant in any collective bargaining situation in which a number of bargaining units have become extremely competitive.

Organizations with two or more dissimilar bargaining units will experience the pressure of competition between the units. One kind of problem that emerges is that bargaining tends to progress at a snail's pace because no unit wants to settle first. Agreements made after the first signed contract seem to be faster. On the other hand, competing bargaining units expect no less than that received by the other units in the organization. In public sector bargaining, much time is wasted playing the waiting game for closure. No unit wants to settle first unless there is some assurance that no other unit will do better.

The union is not without internal pressure. A union has within its ranks various constituencies demanding attention to special needs. Members of the unit sometimes part company during the process of selecting and ranking issues to be negotiated. Even the most homogeneous bargaining units have mini communities of interest, not all of which are represented on the unit's negotiating committee. The pressures involved in determining the priority of bargaining issues that will satisfy the wide range of interests of unit members are often intense. The parties learn that rational compromise and fair trade-offs are necessary if they want to present a strong unified image at the table. Case 14, "Get Me Off the Hook," deals with the crisis that develops when a frantic negotiator attempts to reactivate a priority issue that accidentally fell between the cracks.

The local bargaining unit frequently feels pressure from the parent union to include or exclude specific negotiation issues or to rearrange the priority of bargaining issues. This may come as an honest attempt by the union negotiator to make the local bargaining unit's package of proposals stronger. The union's professional negotiator has access to information regarding agreements and settlements in the surrounding area, and is in a position to compare the local unit's package of proposals with those other settlements. The professional negotiator, cognizant of the union's long-term goals, also plans bargaining strategy and tactics for the eventual realization of those goals.

Comparable status syndrome frequently prevails on both sides of the negotiation table. Each party sifts through contracts of comparable organizations to find agreements that will justify its current position on the issues under consideration. Disagreements intensify when negotiators arbitrarily select favorable bits and pieces of comparable contracts as supporting evidence to justify unreasonable positions. The employees of one bargaining unit may demand the same percentage salary increase as that received by a neighboring bargaining unit, conveniently ignoring the issues that the other unit gave up to get the salary increase. A school district's support staff may be denied a percentage raise equal to the percentage awarded the district's teachers solely because surrounding districts did not award comparable percentages to their support staffs. In time, negotiators learn to recognize and deal with selective comparison data. Thus, authorities suggest that negotiators provide honest and comprehensive comparative reviews, if they are to be used. Constructive bargaining is based on the premise that the same basic facts are available to both negotiating teams.

Related to comparability is the issue of parity. In his publication *Industrial and Labor Relations Terms: A Glossary,* Robert E. Doherty defines *parity* as the "equivalence established between the wage schedules of certain categories of employees. Used commonly in the public sector to describe the ratio maintained between the salaries of police and fire fighters." (Doherty 1989, 25) Webster's Ninth New Collegiate Dictionary definition is broader, "the quality or state of being equal or equivalent." The latter definition allows equivalence of issues other than wage schedules.

Traditionally, the wages and in most cases the benefits of police and fire fighters have been relatively equal. With the advent of collective bargaining for these two uniformed services, the question of parity became more complex. Now each of the service organizations, represented by different unions, negotiated salary and the terms and conditions of employment with an eye to what the other service was getting. It was not always possible for management to synchronize the termination dates of the separate contracts. That led to increased parity problems as the two unions "leapfrogged" one another in settlements. When the termination dates of their two contracts did coincide, one or both of the unions customarily delayed finalizing any agreement until it was known what the other service was getting. In time, this waiting game was alleviated by a form of the "me too" clause, which allowed after-settlement adjustments in certain categories. Complete parity is rarely, if ever, possible because of the many unique job characteristics of police and fire fighters. Case 15, "But the Policemen Get Guns!" illustrates some of these unique job characteristics and the frustration and problems resulting from demands for parity.

Keep the following points in mind when dealing with pressures during collective bargaining:

(1) Recognize that pressure groups generally are not accountable for the consequences of their recommendations. Nor do they have to live with the changes that their demands call for in the same way that the negotiating parties do. The negotiating parties must implement and live with the agreement daily.

(2) Take a proactive role when dealing with pressure groups. Try to predict their needs and requests and to analyze the reasons for them. This will expedite a response to those pressures.

(3) Identify the key communicators in the community pressure groups and keep them informed regarding the issues being negotiated and the progress of negotiations. This must be a joint project based on the cooperation of both negotiating parties.

(4) If negotiation impasse leads to a fact-finding hearing, the fact finder's recommendations should either be published in the community or be made available to interested citizens through management's office. The public will be less inclined to exert pressures if kept informed in an accurate and timely manner.

(5) As a general rule, it is not unreasonable for public employees to expect their incomes to be maintained at about the same levels and to increase at about the same rates as those of like employees in comparable bargaining units. Nor is it unreasonable for management to expect something in return for salary increases and improved working conditions.

(6) The selection of examples from other contracts for comparison purposes during the negotiation process must be relevant and fair.

(7) Accept the fact that it is impossible to realize complete parity with all factions during negotiations.

THE MAYOR SAID...

Dr. Joseph Benson glanced at the golf-ball-shaped clock on his desk as he continued speaking into the phone. "Listen, Ed, it's 10:25 and I've got five minutes to get to my meeting with the board committee. Thanks for the invitation; I'll see you at lunch on Monday." Dr. Benson gathered together the files he had been working on in preparation for the meeting with the school board's negotiation committee and Betty Hill. Betty is the school district's business manager and chief negotiator during bargaining with the Wood Lake Support Personnel Association. As Joe walked through the quiet corridor, he reflected, Ed has heard that we are near settlement with the support personnel association. I'll bet that's the reason for our luncheon meeting on Monday. He will be disappointed, I fear.

DR. JOSEPH BENSON, SUPERINTENDENT OF SCHOOLS

Joe Benson is in his tenth year as superintendent of the Wood Lake Central School District. The forty-five-year-old educator began his teaching career as a business instructor in a small Nebraska school system. In his fifth year, he was invited by the board to apply for the high school principal's position. During his seven years in that position, Joe completed the requirements for the doctorate degree in school administration at the University of Iowa. He turned down a faculty appointment offer by the university to accept the superintendency at Wood Lake. Someday he would try college teaching. Joe looked forward to the challenge of the chief executive officer position in a city school district.

THE BOARD'S COMMITTEE MEETING

Joe Benson entered the boardroom just down the hall from his office and greeted Carl Latella, president of the Wood Lake school board, and Betty Hill. Another member of the school board—the fourth member of the negotiation committee—was not able to attend. As Joe arranged his files on the table in front of him, he noticed that Betty seemed to scrutinize his every move impatiently.

Joe looked up as Betty said, "Just before I came in here, I had a call from Dean Lee that you'd better know about."

Dean Lee is the Wood Lake city attorney and represents the city in collective bargaining with public employees' unions.

Betty continued, "Dean asked if it was true that we are prepared to offer the nonteaching staff an 8 percent increment each year of the two-year contract."

"How did he know that?" asked Superintendent Benson.

"That's what I asked him, and he just said that Mayor Hayes had heard it. The reason for his call was to ask if we would hold off settlement with the association for a week or so."

"Why, for God's sake?" asked Carl.

"If we settle with the association for 8 percent," Betty replied, "the city will feel enormous pressure to offer city employees the same raise. Our nonteaching employees have generally been considered similar in economic status to city workers in the Municipal Maintenance Union. The average salaries of the two groups are currently about the same, and the salaries have been comparable for many years. Our school district and the city call on the same labor market for these employees, who have similar skills and training. The city is very much concerned that our school district employees will jump ahead of city employees if we give this raise.

"Actually, the city is hoping that its police and professional fire fighters will settle for an 8 percent salary increase. Dean Lee said that they do not intend to offer the maintenance employees that much. Thus, they want to settle the maintenance union contract before we settle this contract. I told Dean that I was opposed to any kind of deal but that I would inform you of the city's concern at our meeting today."

"That accounts for the call I had from Mayor Hayes just before this meeting," said Superintendent Benson. "He invited me to lunch on Monday but did not offer any particular reason."

Carl Latella turned to Betty and said, "Your answer to Dean was correct. We don't want any part in that kind of business. If we agree today that we ought to offer the 8 percent salary increase to our employees, I think we should make that offer in our meeting next week and hope that it will provide the closure we are looking for."

"I agree," Joe responded. "I'm not sure the 8 percent offer, along with our other counterproposals, will settle the contract. I think our employees might accept that, but Walt Baker is trying to hold out for the 10 percent that our teaching staff is scheduled to receive."

Walter Baker is the regional senior negotiator for the union and represents the local at the bargaining table.

The district committee meeting lasted another hour, during which a proposal incorporating all of the unsettled issues evolved. It included an 8 percent salary increase.

THE LUNCHEON MEETING

Joe Benson considered himself lucky to find a parking place almost directly in front of the Green Gables Cafe. He put a dime in the parking meter for one-hour parking and entered the cafe. Mayor Ed Hayes, seated at a table for four in a remote corner of the large dining area, was intently studying the menu as Joe approached.

"Hello Ed; sorry I'm late."

"It's just as well—I arrived only a few minutes ago, myself."

A waitress appeared, took their orders, gathered the menus, and left. Wood Lake's two highest-ranking public administrators exchanged small talk about family, vacations, and, of course, golf. The two men were avid golfers, members of the same country club, and occasional golfing partners. After the waitress served coffee, Ed decided to begin the business at hand.

"Joe, one of the reasons I asked you to meet with me is the problem we are having right now with our maintenance union. The word is out that the school district is ready to offer an 8 percent salary increase to its nonteaching group. If that happens, the city is in a real bind because the maximum we are prepared to offer our maintenance people is 5 percent and no additional benefits of any kind. Some members of our city council think our offer is overly generous because employees in the plants around here—employees who are similar to ours—are receiving only 2 or 3 percent raises. How did you get your board to go along with the 8 percent raise?"

"Actually, that figure has not been approved yet by our board nor has it been offered to the employees. However, during the months of negotiation, most of our board members came to realize that our nonteaching salaries are considerably lower than those paid to comparable employees in area school districts. We know that the wages of this group are about the same as those of your city maintenance employees. We are constantly reminded of that fact by one of our board members, who wants us to wait until you settle. He wants us to offer the same raise that you settle for."

"That's exactly what we want you to do—wait, I mean," Ed interrupted. "Betty told Dean she was not in favor of our suggestion to put off your negotiation session scheduled for this week, so we could have a chance to settle first. Did she speak for the district?"

"She did," replied Joe. "This was confirmed at our most recent meeting. What I'm about to tell you is confidential. If we can settle Thursday night with the package we are prepared to offer, which includes an 8 percent wage increase, we will. You must remember that our teachers are set for a 10 percent wage increase. Walt Baker says that his union members won't settle for anything less than that. We think they will. I'm sorry if this complicates your situation."

"I'm sorry, too," said Ed, "because, indeed, our case becomes more complex if you settle. You should know that you and the school board may be in for sharp criticism by several city council members who consider recent school budgets extravagant. These same critics believe that the public would vote your budgets down if they had the opportunity."

"I doubt that our school board members will be intimidated by the city council. The board is confident of its public support."

"Well, so be it," said Ed as he pushed his chair back from the table and picked up the check. "Maybe you won't settle Thursday night."

"Of course, that's possible," responded Joe. "Thanks for the lunch. I'll keep in touch."

As they left the Green Gables, the two administrators agreed to team up for golf more often.

THE IMPASSE

Superintendent Benson knocked on the door of the teachers' lounge and entered. "We're ready anytime you people are. Join us at your convenience."

Walter Baker replied, "Thank you; we will be there in a few minutes."

As Joe Benson closed the door and headed toward the boardroom, Walter turned to Carol Zurek, president of the local association, and said, "Are we agreed then on the strategy we discussed last night? If we go that way, we are taking a calculated risk."

Douglas Waldrup, senior head custodian and member of the employees' negotiating team, replied, "I say we go for it. We can always back off."

"I'm not sure we can," said Carol Zurek. "If both of you are convinced that we should give it a try, I'm willing to go along. As I mentioned last night, though, I'm a bit uneasy about not checking with some of our members first. Most of our people seemed willing to settle in the 8 percent range if we can gain some of the other benefits we now feel are within reach."

Walter ignored the note of skepticism and said, "Well, if we are agreed then, let's send up the trial balloon." With that, he led the trio out the door and toward the boardroom.

After an exchange of the usual amenities, the members of each negotiating team assumed their usual places at the board table.

Betty Hill opened the proceedings, "At our last meeting, the association presented a proposal that the district wanted time to consider. Given the lateness of the hour and the extensiveness of the proposal (it addressed all unsettled issues), we agreed to recess and meet again on this date. We will respond to each of the issues in the order presented by the association at our last meeting.

"The association requests two additional paid holidays for its members: Martin Luther King, Jr., Day and Patriots Day. The district is willing to allow one additional paid holiday, to be selected by the members of the association.

"The district is not willing to increase the health insurance benefits of the part-time teachers' aides and bus monitors as requested by the association. Present benefits equal or surpass those offered to like employees in every district in this three-county area. The data we have confirm that fact. We ask the association to withdraw this proposal.

"The district will approve a 5 percent increase in longevity payments for both the ten-year and the fifteen-year employees. The district will not further consider the 10 percent increase requested by the association.

"In the matter of wage increases, the district offers an 8 percent wage increase each year of the two-year contract. Although that is 2 percent less than the 10 percent requested by the association, it is also 2 percent more than what has been offered by any district to date in the three-county area.

"The district agrees with the association's proposal to have the new agreement retroactive to July 1."

Betty paused and then continued, "We sincerely hope that the association will view this district counterproposal as a fair and equitable compromise. Three of the four unsettled issues have once again been reconsidered and increased. The district is making a sincere effort to offer an attractive package that will result in a new agreement. We assume that the association will want a caucus to consider this offer." With a look of confidence, Betty pushed her chair back, stood, and headed for the table holding refreshments at the far end of the room. Others got up to follow her.

"No, we don't need a caucus to respond to the district's offer," Walt announced.

Betty stopped pouring her coffee and glanced at Superintendent Benson, not sure how to react to the unexpected statement by the association's negotiator.

"I'll be right there," she said in a faint voice.

When everyone was again seated around the table, Walt said, "We anticipated some of the counterproposals you have made today and prepared our own counterproposal. We accept your offer provided that you agree to a wage increase of 10 percent each year of the contract. I don't think we should have to repeat all the arguments already presented to justify our 10 percent request. If you do this, we have a new contract."

Betty glanced at her team members for a moment and then replied, "Well, we will need a caucus to discuss this offer."

"No we won't!" shouted the board president, Carl Latella. "I'm opposed to any salary increase in excess of our last offer of 8 percent. I can tell you the board will not approve anything over what has already been offered. I think we have been extremely fair with you in these proceedings. In my opinion, you have not provided a reasonable basis for a 10 percent wage increase. If you don't accept this offer, I am in favor of ending these negotiations."

As Carl spoke, his face reddened noticeably, giving evidence of his increasing anger and frustration. When he finished, he began gathering and stacking his materials in preparation to leave.

During the moments of silence following Carl's outburst, Betty's eyes, fixed on Joe, pleaded for help.

Joe broke the silence, "Why don't we take a ten-minute break and then decide the steps to take."

"I don't think a caucus at this time will serve any purpose," said Walt, staring at Joe. "Your attitude and last counterproposal confirm the rumor we heard that Mayor Ed Hayes has been assured that you will not settle with us until the city has signed an agreement with its maintenance workers. So what's the point of going on with this charade? We think you eventually will..."

"That is not true," interrupted Joe. "There is no agreement with the mayor or anyone else."

"We heard that Dean Lee called Betty last week with just such a proposal. And we know that earlier this week Mayor Hayes had lunch with you, Dr. Benson, and that these negotiations were discussed then. We believe that until this deal was struck, the school district intended to offer a 10 percent wage increase. You now offer 8 percent because you know that offer will stall these proceedings, and that's what you have agreed to do. I want you to know that we are considering filing an improper practice charge against the school district."

With that, Walt Baker and the two association representatives walked out.

THE MAYOR SAID...

Questions for Discussion

1. What would you select as the most important factors in this situation? Why?
2. Do you think Betty Hill is the appropriate person to serve as district negotiator with this group of employees?
3. Why didn't the association's representatives react to the district's counterproposal in the way Betty anticipated they would?
4. How did the association's members hear about the city's request to stall negotiations?
5. What effect did Carl Latella's outburst have on the outcome of this bargaining session?
6. What does the association hope to gain by its tactics in this case?
7. What immediate course of action would you advise Superintendent Benson to take?

CASE TWELVE

CAUGHT IN THE MIDDLE

Robert Lund rearranged the stack of papers on the table in front of him, anticipating an end to the meeting. He did not look up when Dr. Frank Anslom, superintendent of the Webster Consolidated Schools, directly addressed him, "Bob, we hope that you and the other teachers will give our proposal very serious consideration. Not only will all teachers get a nice little bonus, but we can have every teacher in our system earning at least the mean salary of comparable colleagues in our Northwest Region."

Robert now glanced up and replied, "Well, you realize, Frank, that the proposal you made was not expected. We thought the district would agree to divide the State Merit Award money equally among our bargaining unit members. That's what all the schools in our region are doing."

As Frank stood up to leave, he said, "The school board is really determined to use this money to correct some salary inequities. Anyway, let's talk about it at our next meeting, two weeks from today."

Robert and Ivan Smith, another teacher on the negotiation committee, wandered off in the direction of the faculty lounge. Handing Ivan a cup of coffee, Robert asked, "What did you think of that?"

"I really don't know what to think. The proposal will surely get enthusiastic support from our first-, second-, and third-year teachers, who will receive the additional money. The question is, how will it be received by the rest of the teachers, who are counting on an even distribution of the award? Hell, some of them have even spent it."

"I've heard that too. This really puts us in a box. It appears to me that the district wants to use this award money to make up for the low starting salary it set for teachers the last three or four years, and that ticks me off. Anyway, I'll call a meeting of the whole negotiating committee next week.

I think we'd better keep this to ourselves until the meeting. Let's call it a day."

THE STATE MERIT AWARDS

In 1983, the National Commission on Excellence in Education issued its report *A Nation at Risk*. This document, which proclaimed that the nation was undergoing "an act of unthinking, unilateral, educational disarmament," received much publicity and wide distribution. State legislatures, state boards of education, and state education departments responded by creating hundreds of reform proposals, including merit pay schemes, career ladders for teachers, longer school calendars, and higher certification standards.

One of the reforms dreamed up by the state legislature is the State Merit Awards System. The intent was to recognize and reward the best teachers in the state. Each school district receives a block grant of funds to be used as performance rewards for deserving teachers. However, the law also stipulates that the method of distribution of these funds is a matter for negotiation between the district and the teachers' association, independent of the regular contract negotiation. Ninety-five percent of the school districts in the state negotiated a distribution system that divides the money equally among all teachers. Incompetent teachers receive the same "bonus" that the best teachers receive. Responding to criticism of the whole procedure, legislators merely say that the awards were intended to reward the best teachers in each school system, not provide a bonus for all. Legislators are not about to challenge the unions on this one.

THE PROPOSALS

The Webster school district's proposal for distribution of State Merit Award funds calls for: (a) payments to first-, second-, and third-year teachers that would raise their salaries to equal the average salaries of teachers in districts in the Northwest Region who also are in their first, second, and third years of teaching, and (b) distribution of equal shares of the balance of the award money among all the teachers. A survey conducted by Superintendent Anslom shows that teachers at Webster except those on the first three steps of the salary schedule are above the region mean for salary. Recognizing that this plan does not reward merit as intended by the legislators, Anslom, nevertheless, considers it beneficial to the lowest-paid teachers and to the district. It may help to retain energetic, young teachers and also to provide a more attractive starting salary. He estimates that about 80 percent of the fund will be available for across-the-board distribution.

The Webster Teachers Association (WTA) vehemently objects to the district's plan for allocating the merit awards. The WTA proposes that the award monies be divided equally among all Webster teachers, with no special concessions. The association argues that, under the district's plan, the teachers with the least experience and tenure will receive the largest shares of the award. And besides, the State and Regional Teachers Associations recommend that the awards be divided equally among all the teachers in the district.

THE REGIONAL MEETING

Soon after the State Merit Awards were announced, local district teachers' association presidents were invited to a Northwest Region meeting to discuss strategy for negotiating the distribution process, as mandated by the law. The workshop leaders circulated a report on a task force study by the Association for Supervision and Curriculum Development (ASCD), which set the agenda for the discussion. According to the study, merit pay and teacher career ladders produce political confrontation, not better schools. These two remedies are a "simplistic approach to a complex problem," says the study. Based on the discussion at the meeting, it appeared that few, if any, school districts intended to challenge the assumptions in the ASCD report. The consensus of the workshop participants was to distribute the award funds across the board.

THE NEGOTIATION COMMITTEE

Robert Lund called a meeting of the seven-member teachers' negotiation committee for 7:00 P.M. in the high school faculty lounge. He did not send out an agenda before the meeting because he did not want the districts' proposal to be discussed by the teachers before his committee had a chance to address it. If the committee agreed on a course of action at this meeting, he had another week before the next negotiation session with the board to call a general faculty meeting, if that proved necessary. He hoped a general meeting would not be necessary. Ten minutes before he was set to leave his house for the meeting, his wife called him to the phone.

"Bob," said the familiar voice, "this is Don up at Dow City. How are things?" Don Waldrup, the man on the other end of the phone, is president of the County Teachers Association.

"Fine, Don. Say, listen, I can't talk right now—I'm on my way to a meeting."

"I know you are. I understand your school board came up with a new wrinkle for distributing award money. What is your committee going to do?"

"I really don't know, Don; that's why we're meeting tonight. By the way, how did you hear about this?"

"Apparently you have a board member who tells all. Listen, Bob, I'm calling to urge you and the committee to hold the line. If your district distributes the award money using a different formula..."

Bob interrupted, "Don, I really must go. I honestly don't know what our group will do, but, in any event, it will have to be our decision. I'll let you know what happens."

As Bob drove up to the school, he noticed the unusually large number of cars on the lot, most of which he recognized. When he walked into the teachers' lounge, Ivan, his negotiation partner, confirmed his supposition about the reason for the full parking lot, saying, "Since you weren't here, I decided to ask the group to move to the cafeteria. Many of the teachers are here, including practically all of our new teachers. The word is out. One of the first-year teachers asked me if we were really against the school board's proposal. Are we going to hold a committee meeting with that mob looking on?"

As they walked down the hall toward the cafeteria, Bob told Ivan about his phone call. They paused at the door, listening for a minute to an angry verbal exchange already in progress. As they opened the door to enter, Bob displayed a nervous smile and said, "I wish I knew how to back away from this one."

CAUGHT IN THE MIDDLE

Questions for Discussion

1. What is your opinion of the State Merit Awards System passed by the state legislature?
2. How do you feel about the district's proposal for distribution of merit award funds?
3. Why did no one challenge the ASCD report findings?
4. Should Bob have handled the whole situation differently?
5. What course of action would you advise Bob to take when he confronts the teachers who appeared at the committee meeting? Why?
6. What other issues does this case pose for you?

CASE THIRTEEN

BUT WHAT ABOUT...?

Ed Morgan placed his coffee cup on the coaster beside the appointment calendar on his desk. He flipped the calendar page to see how this day and a new week would begin. He groaned when he saw that in ten minutes he had a meeting with Dick Sanders, president of the Plymouth County Highway Workers Union. That usually spelled trouble.

As Morgan reached to push the intercom button, his secretary, Cathy, entered and said, "I missed you when you came in because I went to records to pull Joe Decker's file. You may need it when Dick Sanders gets here. He called first thing this morning, insisting on seeing you right away. I gave him your first appointment. Is that OK?"

"Yes, I'll have to see him," responded Morgan. "Did he say what he wanted? What about this Joe Decker?"

"All he would tell me was that he wanted to talk to you about Joe Decker. I'll let you know when he gets here," said Cathy as she closed the door between offices.

Ed Morgan noted his office imprint, *Office of Director of Personnel, Plymouth County*, on the outside of Decker's file as he opened it. As he scrutinized the documents in the folder, he recalled previous disciplinary problems involving Decker. His examination was interrupted by Cathy, who told him that Dick Sanders was waiting.

Sanders declined the offer of a cup of coffee and seemed anxious to get on with the business at hand. As usual, he didn't beat around the bush. "Joe Decker was suspended this morning when he reported for work, and I want him reinstated."

"Do you want to tell me why he was suspended?" asked Morgan. "John Murray doesn't suspend workers just for coming to work late." John Murray is superintendent of the highway department.

"Decker was on call Saturday because of the snowstorm warning. When he was called Saturday to work the blizzard, he said he couldn't report because he was sick. Then at 2:00 A.M. Sunday morning, he got picked up for fighting outside a local bar, and he was booked. The damn fool took a poke at the arresting officer. When he reported for work this morning, John suspended him, pending a hearing. I'd like you to call John."

"And tell him what?" said Morgan angrily. "You know as well as I that this is at least the second time Decker has pulled this. He has been written up once before on the same kind of charge. Last year he had a thirty-day suspension for drinking on the job. I can't think of any reason to call Murray."

"Then I'll give you one!" shot back Sanders, "Equity, fairness, justice—call it what you want. A month or so ago one of the sheriff's deputies called in sick and was caught out drinking. It wasn't his first time, and he was not suspended. And there have been other incidents, too. Workers in the sheriff's office, county clerk's office, and even those in the county education offices seem to operate according to a different set of rules." As he got up to leave, he warned, "If this ends up in a grievance hearing, I'm going to press that issue."

"Do what you want," said Morgan. "I will call John Murray and talk to him, but I will not ask him to drop the charges. I'll get back to you when I have scheduled the hearing."

Morgan stared at the slammed door after Sanders left and thought to himself, How will the arbitrator deal with our dual personnel policies if it comes to that? He knew the answer.

PLYMOUTH COUNTY

Plymouth County government is not unlike most county governments in other parts of the country. An elected county board of nine part-time legislators serves as the legislative, policy-making body. The statutes do not provide for a single elected executive authority. The president of the county board takes on the role of chief executive officer. When the state allowed collective bargaining for all public employees, personnel matters became too complex and burdensome for the current board president, Bill Fraser. He prevailed upon the board to hire a personnel director. Ed Morgan has served in that position for three years.

During his first year in office, Morgan convinced Bill Fraser and the board to approve a broad personnel administration policy to be administered by his office. The new administrative document described the policies, procedures, and practices to be used when dealing with employees and their problems.

Morgan modeled his policy statement after that of the County Education Intermediate Unit (I.U.). Although teachers and school administrators made up most of the I.U. employees, the I.U. Support Personnel Union included many of the same classifications of workers as in the other county organizations. Neither the new director nor the board realized that the board could not delegate administrative authority it did not have. Before the announcement of the revised countywide personnel policy, the authority of county legislators to develop and implement personnel policies for all county employees had not been tested. The county legislators and Morgan soon learned that, unlike the County Education Intermediate Unit, they did not have exclusive policy-making and administrative authority. They shared that authority with the three elected county officials.

State statutes confer extensive personnel powers over three county departments to the three elected county officials: the county sheriff, the county clerk, and the county treasurer. It was not long before Morgan learned just how extensive those powers are.

An employee in the county clerk's office filed a grievance when she was denied a personal day. Personnel policy set by Mary Jansen, the county clerk, called for forty-eight hours' notice to take a personal day unless it was an emergency. The employee did not have an emergency and was denied the leave when her request came with less than one day's notice. Because the recently promulgated county personnel policy did not require the two-day advance notice for a personal day, the employee filed a grievance with the personnel director. Two days before the scheduled hearing, Mary Jansen asked to see Morgan. She brought a friend, who just happened to be a state arbitrator. It was then that Morgan learned that when personnel policies of the county board conflict with personnel policies of elected county officials, the state tends to give preference to the policies of elected officials.

This is not necessarily the case, however, when dealing with appointed county officials and their personnel. In addition to the three departments headed by elected officials, there are five county departments that are headed by administrators appointed by the county board: Commissioner of Social Services, Director of the Health Department, Superintendent of Highways, Director of Probation, and Zoning Director. Because these department heads are appointed by the county board, it was assumed that their employees surely would be covered by the personnel policies adopted by the board. However, the appointed administrators had operated with their own policies for so long that they tended to ignore the board's directive. Working for the county was a frustrating experience for many employees, including the supervisors. They came to depend on the unions to provide means of developing working relationships with their bosses. The union representative often led employees through the bureaucratic maze and was able to find a supervisor who had both the managerial responsibility and formal authority to resolve a grievance.

MORGAN'S SOLUTION

Ed Morgan picked up the telephone on the second ring. "Morgan here," he said.

"Hi Ed. I hear we have another case with Joe Decker," said Bill Fraser. "I just had a call from Dick Sanders, who gave me the whole story. In my opinion, Joe Decker ought to be fired. Unfortunately, Sanders has a point. That sheriff's deputy case and several others he pointed out in the clerk's office will hurt us if we end up in arbitration on this one."

"I hope you're not about to ask that I change my mind on the Decker case, because..."

"Hell no!" interrupted Fraser. "I'm in complete agreement with your decision to support John Murray on this. I guess I'm just discouraged by the thought that we could lose this one because of the inequities built into our system and our confusing authority structure. When we created your office of personnel director, we county legislators sincerely believed that this office would be able to consolidate our personnel policies and reduce friction. That has not proved to be true. Hell, the unions have a better sense of how this county government works than the managers do.

"We negotiate with only four unions in the county and we get through that without a lot of trouble. Our problems seem to crop up between negotiations. Due to our inconsistencies, we have too many employee grievances. Management is losing too many of those. We need to do something."

"I've been giving all of this a great deal of thought the last couple of days and I have several ideas I'd like to bounce off you," responded Morgan. "I'm convinced that the form and structure of the county government is not going to change in the immediate future. But I think we can do some things to reduce the pressures used by the four unions in playing one management policy against another. It will take a little time, but I think it's worth a try. When can we get together?"

"How about in five minutes? I'm in my office here in the courthouse and I can be right down," said Fraser.

Three minutes later, the president of the county board bounced into Morgan's office and said, "OK, Houdini, tell me how we're going to turn this around!"

BUT WHAT ABOUT...?

Questions for Discussion

1. What issues are involved in this case?
2. What circumstances led Sanders to conclude that Morgan would reverse John Murray's decision to suspend Decker?
3. What are the major problems with county government as described in this case?
4. Why would you expect to find strong unions in Plymouth County?
5. Why was management losing most of the arbitrated grievances in Plymouth County?
6. If you were Morgan, how would you respond to Fraser's final question? What suggestions would you make to reform government policy and procedures in Plymouth County? Why?

CASE FOURTEEN

GET ME OFF THE HOOK

PINE BLUFF INDEPENDENT SCHOOL DISTRICT
InterOffice Memorandum

TO: Mr. Robert Maxwell
President
Pine Bluff Teachers Association

FROM: Mr. Karl Hunter
Superintendent

RE: Contract Negotiations

As I promised at 3 A.M. this morning, when we finally reached closure of our contract negotiations, I have summarized the final settlements under the two classifications we discussed.

The following issues were signed off on during previous negotiation sessions. Both parties have copies of those signed agreements.

(1) Building faculty meetings will be limited to two per month.
(2) The high school band and chorus instructors will be compensated for summer work per the schedule submitted by the association.
(3) The number of sick days and personal days will remain the same as in the current contract.

(4) Teachers will report to homerooms twenty minutes earlier, as proposed in the district's revised schedule and calendar.

The following revisions of the current contract were agreed to last night:

(1) The duration of the contract will be two years.
(2) Teachers' salaries will be increased by 10 percent the first year and by 8 percent the second year of the two-year contract.
(3) The dental plan proposed by the association will be added to the current medical coverage plan, and the prescription co-pay will be raised from one dollar to three dollars.
(4) The district has agreed to binding arbitration as the final step in the grievance procedure.

All other district and association proposals have been withdrawn.

I believe that the above summary accurately reflects our final agreement. If you concur, I can send the necessary information and documents to have the new contract drawn up.

I am pleased that we were able to avoid the impasse that seemed imminent only a few days ago. Apparently both parties entered the final round of negotiation in a spirit of compromise and were determined to arrive at a final settlement.

I look forward to hearing from you after you have had the opportunity to review the above summary.

cc: Mr. Milt Hawley
       President
       Pine Bluff Board of Education

PINE BLUFF INDEPENDENT SCHOOL DISTRICT
InterOffice Memorandum

TO: **Karl Hunter**

FROM: **Bob Maxwell**

RE: **Negotiations**

Thank you for the summary of negotiated changes in the current contract. The modifications listed in your memorandum are correct.

However, we do have a problem. The association's proposal to increase district reimbursement for graduate credit hours was not mentioned as a part of our final settlement. In fact, my notes of that last meeting indicate that the issue was not even discussed as we put together the synopsis of issues ending that marathon session.

I have no idea how this issue was lost as a part of our economic package. We did discuss it. My notes show that one of your counterproposals requested that this issue be dropped, but we did not accept that. We did stress the high priority this issue has for our increasing number of young faculty who are working toward permanent certification. I doubt that a contract would be ratified by our members without some significant adjustment of these payments. You may recall that our principal argument for this increase was that this payment has not been increased over the past ten years.

Can we get together and talk about this? I will be grateful to hear any suggestions you may have for resolving this dilemma.

PINE BLUFF INDEPENDENT SCHOOL DISTRICT
InterOffice Memorandum

TO: **Bob Maxwell**

FROM: **Karl Hunter**

RE: **Negotiation Problem**

I am astonished and disappointed to learn that we may not indeed have a tentative contract agreement. In one sense we do, because you signed the memorandum of understanding that concluded our negotiations, pending ratification by our respective constituencies. On the other hand, if the teachers do not ratify our negotiated agreement, we do have a serious problem.

My negotiation notes indicate that your proposal to increase payments for graduate course credits was not discussed during the last three or four meetings. I have no idea why. I expect it's because you did not advance that proposal as part of the economic package that we eventually put together. I can tell you that the board would not have authorized the 18 percent salary increase in addition to a substantial increase in the payments for graduate credit. And then there is the binding arbitration issue. From the very beginning of negotiations, the board was determined to hold the line on that one. You will recall how vehement the board president was. No one was more surprised than

I when several board members decided to concede this issue if it would settle the contract. Even then, the other board members were not happy with our decision.

I suggest we leave well enough alone. We both know how difficult it was to get the agreement we have. To open it up again is to risk prolonged negotiation and inevitable impasse and conciliation procedures. I advise you to find a way to explain the situation to the teachers.

cc: Milt Hawley

PINE BLUFF INDEPENDENT SCHOOL DISTRICT
InterOffice Memorandum

TO: **Karl Hunter**

FROM: **Bob Maxwell**

RE: **Negotiation Problem**

A member of our teachers' negotiating team has come upon a trail that explains our mysteriously lost proposal. At one point during a negotiation caucus, we decided to group the increase for graduate course credit proposal with the medical insurance and several other issues as a mini package. When the district didn't buy that, we regrouped all our economic items and, in the process, forgot to include the graduate course credit issue. Unfortunately, our negotiating team is made up of senior faculty members who would not benefit by those increased payments. Thus, without that personal interest on the part of senior faculty members, this issue was allowed to fall through the cracks as we summarized the final proposals.

Again, I emphasize that this is a sensitive and high-priority item for our younger faculty who must continue working toward the master's degree for permanent certification. They currently pay up to $1,000 for a three-credit course at the local university.

The primary responsibility for this careless, albeit honest, error lies with me. I should have checked the agreement more carefully before signing it. Because I didn't, I sense a responsibility to do what I can to persuade management to reconsider this issue. I feel a special urgency to succeed in these negotiations because we teachers suggested negotiating this year without outside help.

What, if anything, will influence the district board to again address this association proposal to double the current amount paid for graduate-credit courses?

I will be grateful for anything you can do personally to help me off the hook.

PINE BLUFF INDEPENDENT SCHOOL DISTRICT
InterOffice Memorandum

TO: **Mr. Milt Hawley**
           President
           Board of Education

FROM: **Karl Hunter**

RE: **Recommendation for resolving the Negotiation Stalemate**

The teachers' association continues to press for board reconsideration of its request to double current district payment for approved graduate credit hours. The association has not taken my suggestion to withdraw the proposal in light of our presumed tentative settlement.

During our recent telephone conversation, you suggested I prepare my recommendation for the solution to this problem. Assuming that neither party desires to declare a formal impasse requiring the appointment of a state mediator, I suggest the following:

GET ME OFF THE HOOK

Questions for Discussion

1. What are the major issues in this case?
2. How is it possible for priority issues to get lost or forgotten during negotiations? Explain.
3. Why is this particular lost proposal a very sensitive issue for the association?
4. How can incidents like this be avoided during negotiation?

5. What are the advantages and disadvantages of approving the association's request to increase payment for graduate course credits after closure? Why?
6. If you were Karl Hunter, what would be your recommendation to the Board of Education in the last memorandum? Why?

BUT THE POLICEMEN GET GUNS!

City Attorney Dean Lee pitched the untidy stack of papers into the open briefcase, whacked the latch shut, and walked out of the council room into the lobby of Wood Lake City Hall. He was waiting at the elevator when a familiar voice called, "Hey, Dean, Chief McCarthy tells me you had a rough day." He turned to see Mayor Ed Hayes hurrying through the almost empty lobby to catch up to him before the elevator door opened.

Dean replied, "*That* is an understatement."

"The chief says there is little chance his fire fighters will settle until they see how the police make out with their contract. Is that so?"

"Probably, but I expect the fire fighters to declare an impasse as a stall tactic, if necessary."

As they entered the empty elevator, Mayor Hayes asked, "Do you have a few minutes or so now to fill me in? I would like to hear the details of today's meeting."

"Yeah, it won't take much time to fill you in. We had the same old arguments with some new twists."

"Is a parity provision in the fire fighters' contract still the underlying issue?"

"It sure is! My God, at one point in today's exchange, we were emphatically reminded that, in addition to the other inequities, the police get lunch and guns!"

THE CITY

Wood Lake is generally thought of as a small midwestern city with a rather stable population of approximately 26,500 souls. The population is stable primarily because Wood Lake serves as the shopping center for a wide area with a population of about 350,000. The nearest larger city is Ponca, which is more than 100 miles to the south. Two large shopping malls and a thriving downtown business district provide well over 300 retail outlets for the area's avid shoppers.

The city has about a dozen industrial plants; the smallest employs eight to ten people, and the largest has a seasonal peak employment of over 400.

The Wood Lake public school system is consistently rated superior by the accrediting agencies and enjoys strong community support. Until this year, the school district has had few labor problems. Last year, the professional staff negotiated a three-year contract that allowed a 10 percent salary increase each year of the contract. The teachers are among the highest paid in the area. Current negotiations with the school district's support staff ground to a halt when the union demanded 10 percent salary increases each year to match what the teachers received.

Two excellent hospitals and a typical public junior college serve the area.

A railroad and a small river subdivide the city into almost three equal areas, each having a self-contained fire fighting unit. Some years ago, a city proposal to close one of the fire stations touched off the only real militant demonstration by the fire fighters. The fire fighters claimed that a flood or a railroad train disaster would leave one part of the city without fire protection. City management eventually withdrew the proposal and renovated the targeted fire station.

THE NEGOTIATORS

Edward Hayes is serving in the second year of his third term as mayor. His predecessor was the first full-time mayor of Wood Lake. There are those who still believe that a full-time mayor is an extravagance that the city can ill afford. Mayor Hayes does not attend negotiation sessions. He prefers the role of unofficial advisor to one or both parties.

Dean Lee was appointed city attorney by Mayor Hayes during his first term. Attorney Lee represents the city in collective bargaining with all public employee unions.

Richard (Dick) McCarthy has served as fire chief for the past thirteen years. He came up through the ranks and is well respected by his department. Chief McCarthy's dislike for the bargaining process, which became law just before his appointment, is no secret. He is an unenthusiastic member of management's fire fighter bargaining team.

Julian Martin is a fire fighter with the rank of lieutenant. He serves as negotiator for the local fire fighters' association and is generally regarded as the most militant of the fire fighters. He replaced Don Blue as negotiator three years ago when Don was appointed captain.

Don Blue is a fire fighter with the rank of captain. Until his promotion three years ago, he represented the fire fighters at the negotiating table. He continues as a member of the negotiation team.

Tony Cass is a fire fighter with five years of service who is serving his first term on the negotiating team.

Martin Good has twelve years' experience as a fire fighter and as a member of the negotiating team. Three years ago, Julian defeated him in the election of a negotiator for the local fire fighters' association.

Jean Wortman, a member of the city council for six years, represents the council on management's negotiation team.

THE MEETING

The negotiation meeting that Ed Hayes and Dean Lee were discussing started on time at 9:00 A.M. on, Wednesday, May 5, in the city council boardroom at City Hall. It was the seventh in the series of bargaining sessions that began during the first week of February. Little progress had been made in the effort to get a successor agreement to the current contract, which expires June 30.

Fire Chief Dick McCarthy called the meeting to order. "I would like to make a few remarks before we begin our formal negotiation session. This morning, during an earlier meeting with me, Mayor Hayes expressed disappointment in our lack of progress to date in negotiations. He asked that I urge both parties to be reasonable and fair during the continuing deliberations. To that end, I wish to express my hope that we can wrap this up with a final agreement today."

Julian Martin, the union negotiator, asked, "Why doesn't 'hiz honor' appear in person to deliver his pep talks? After all, he is only two floors away in this building."

Chief McCarthy replied, "He had to leave for another meeting but will be back in his office this afternoon. He said that he would be available after lunch if we wanted to call on him."

"Well, we all know Ed is available," interrupted Dean Lee, chief negotiator for the city. "Now, let's get on with our business. Allow me to recap the current positions of the parties on the outstanding issues. At the end of the last meeting, management presented a counterproposal, which was not accepted by the union. Thus, as I see it, here is where we are:

"Regarding salary, the union demands a 10 percent increase during each year of the two-year contract, and the city has offered 6 percent the first year and 5 percent the second year of the contract."

Julian interrupted, "We have agreed that we are talking a two-year contract. Is that correct?"

"Yes," responded Dean. "Now, concerning the work schedule, since fire fighters work a forty-two-hour week, the union is asking for some form of compensation for the two additional hours beyond the forty-hour week worked by the police and other city employees. The city, for reasons cited during previous negotiations, is not willing to entertain this proposal.

"Regarding allowances, the union seeks a $100 increase in the clothing allowance and wants to add a meal allowance comparable to what the police now receive. Given the financial impact of the association's other demands, especially salary, we do not accept this.

"The union requests language in the contract that would limit on-duty assignments of fire fighters by management, such as maintenance work. The city reserves the right to assign the duties of all employees. Thus, the city cannot agree to such language. Besides, we are informed that this has not been a problem. Fire fighters are not assigned to maintenance work. When the fire fighters request materials to fix something or touch up a wall, the materials are provided.

"Regarding longevity, the union seeks to remove the twenty-year limit on the period during which the annual longevity payment of $50 per year may be earned. This would eliminate the need to stipulate a maximum longevity payment, currently set at $1,000. The city has turned down this proposal.

"The union also wants a parity provision in the contract so that police and fire fighters will automatically get the salary increments and benefits received by the other unit. The city has denied this proposal.

"The only city proposal, other than salary, left on the table is our proposal to remove the fire fighter captains and lieutenants from this negotiating unit so they may form a unit of their own, as is the case with the police organization. The union has not approved this issue."

"Thank you, Dean," Julian said. "I think that is an accurate summation of where we are now." He continued, "Since the last negotiation session, our committee has met and we have a new mini package for you to consider."

"That's good! We are most anxious to get a revised, reasonable proposal from the union that can be seriously considered," replied Dean. "Let's have it!"

"First of all, I remind you that we know the city has not settled with the police unit. As we have pointed out before, that makes us very wary of committing to a final agreement before contract settlement with the police unless we have a parity provision in our contract. We are tired of playing 'leapfrog' with the police unit. One of us is always trying to 'catch up,' and it usually is our fire fighters' unit because we have settled first. We suspect that the city's rejection of our proposed parity provision is another means of retaliation for our reluctance to merge with the police unit, as suggested by you two years ago. Otherwise, it doesn't make sense. If the police and fire fighters were one unit, as you wanted, we, obviously, would be negotiating comparable benefits and salaries. However, we have not changed in that regard. We want to maintain our independent bargaining unit."

"Can we get on with your revised package proposal?" Dean asked.

"We can. I just wanted to remind you again how absurd it is for you, on the one hand, to push for a merged police and fire fighter unit and, on the other hand, to refuse to consider a parity provision," replied Julian. "Our package is as follows:

"One, salary increments will be 8 percent the first year and 10 percent the second year. We have reduced our first-year request by 2 percent. Even though we believe we deserve a raise equal to what other professionals in the city are getting—for example, the teachers—we are willing to sacrifice in the interest of a settlement.

"Two, fire fighters work an average of forty-two hours per week and police have a forty-hour week. We are not asking for a forty-hour week. We do want compensatory pay, or compensatory time off, or a combination of pay and time off for the extra two hours a week.

"Three, we have not changed our original request for a $100 additional clothing allowance and the same meal allowance now provided to the police.

"Four, since you were not swayed by the language we proposed for a parity provision in the contract, we ask you to propose parity language for our consideration.

"Five, the city must drop its proposal to change unit membership. The members of this unit are unanimous in their determination to keep the unit as is. All fire fighters, including the officers, think of themselves as one family, depending on each other for their safety and sometimes their very lives. This close bond must not be weakened by a separation of members and the inevitable rivalry within ranks.

"Six, if we can come to some agreement on these issues, the association will withdraw its proposal for a change in longevity payments and its on-duty assignments proposal."

The prolonged silence that followed Julian's presentation was broken by Dean. "Well, obviously we need a caucus to consider your comprehensive proposal. One point of clarification before we adjourn. The city is not merely objecting to the language you propose for a parity provision. We object to the whole concept of a 'me too' clause."

THE CAUCUS

With that clarification, Dean led his team across the hall to the jury room. After the door was closed, he turned to face his group. "Well, what do you think?"

Chief McCarthy was the first to speak. "I think we have some major concessions here, and we ought to give serious consideration to this proposal."

"Why, for God's sake?" shouted Jean Wortman. "Do you really consider a drop of 2 percent in salary over the two-year period a major concession? That's still an 18 percent increase over the two years of the contract. The council will never approve that. Most members want a maximum of 12 percent over the two years, and we have already offered 11 percent. I've reminded you people before that my husband got just a 2 percent raise last January, and the year before that he received nothing."

Dean interrupted, "Jean, we have heard that before, and we keep reminding you that we are not negotiating your husband's raise. What did you think of the rest of the package?"

"Well, I can see their point on the work schedule issue—they do work two hours more a week than the police. Chief, I've heard you explain and defend the reason for the forty-two-hour week, so I guess we know where you stand. If we were to compensate them for the extra two hours, which system would be the most beneficial to the department?"

"I'd suggest we use the same procedure we now have for compensating fire fighters for holidays they are unable to take," replied the chief, "That is, try to arrange compensatory time off and, if that is impossible, prorate pay for the extra hours. In most cases, I think we can arrange time off."

Dean agreed, "I think we can go with that if the other issues fall into place. I did not expect them to give up the longevity issue. However, I am not surprised by their offer to drop the on-duty assignment proposal. They know as well as we do that recent rulings stipulate that a demand relating to assignment of work is not a mandatory subject of negotiation. If it were, it could prevent management from assigning essential duties to employees. Besides, the chief has been reminding all of us that this has not been a problem."

"Then, why do they bring it up?" asked Jean.

Dean answered, "We really don't know. It was probably intended as a throw-away item that could be traded for a higher-priority issue."

"And we now know what those are," the chief added. "I'd suggest we compromise: allow the additional $100 clothing allowance and not add a meal allowance."

"That's a compromise, Chief, but I can't buy it," said Dean. "Currently, both the police and the fire fighters get a $400 clothing allowance. If we give the fire fighters another $100, you know the police unit will demand the same. That's a 25 percent increase. We should refuse to accept this whole request."

"I agree," added Jean.

"OK, Chief?" asked Dean.

"I guess," replied the chief, "but I don't think we're getting much closer to a settlement."

"I assume we have not changed our minds about a parity provision in the contract." Dean waited for an affirmative sign from his team and then continued, "That leaves our unit membership proposal. My opinion is that we don't stand much of a chance on this one. Our local Professional Fire Fighters Association is adamant in its determination to maintain one negotiating unit for all fire fighters with the exception of the chief, of course. Jean, has the city council softened its position on this issue?"

"I think it has, Dean," Jean replied. "As you know, for years this has been a priority issue with many of our council members. They feel that the lieutenants and the captains should form their own negotiating unit as the police do. Many of us believe that the role of supervisory personnel in the fire department is blurred and confused by the current arrangement. On the other hand, we are assured by the chief that this is not the case. I think the council will ratify a contract without this provision provided that the other points at issue are acceptable."

"Then I believe we now have a counteroffer to propose, provided that we decide on the salary increment. Their last request is 8 percent the first year and 10 percent the second. Our last offer is 6 percent the first year and 5 percent the second. The guidelines provided by the council limit salary increments to no more than 14 percent over the two-year period. Jean has pointed out, though, that the council would rather settle for 12 percent, total. I propose that we adjust an additional 2 percent as they did and offer 7 percent the first year and 6 percent the second. That will allow us 1 percent for another move if we want to. Agreed?"

Jean murmured a very reluctant yes. The chief nodded affirmatively, as Dean knew he would.

"Good," Dean said. "Shall we then return to the council room and get this thing settled?"

THE COUNTERPROPOSAL

The members of both teams took their places around the table and fixed their attention on Dean. He put the papers in front of him in order, made several notes on them, and opened the meeting, saying, "We have a counterproposal that we hope you will find acceptable. I will address the issues in the same order as your last proposal. However, you must realize that this is a package offer. Although individual items may be discussed, our proposed compromises are valid only as a part of the whole.

"We appreciate your ceding 2 percent in your increment request and, in the same spirit of cooperation, raise our offer a like 2 percent. We now offer a salary increment of 7 percent the first year and 6 percent the second year.

"The city is willing to approve your work schedule adjustment proposal in the language that you propose. We can confirm that language before settlement.

"Your request for an additional clothing allowance and a meal allowance is not acceptable. And the city is not willing to include a parity provision in the new contract. We can provide the rationale for this position again if you want, but we have been over this ground before.

"The city is willing to withdraw its proposal for a change in the fire fighters' bargaining unit membership. This decision may be difficult to sell to the council, but we are willing to try. Since you recalled your proposals dealing with longevity and on-duty assignments, that about sums it up."

Julian Martin continued to scribble notes for two or three minutes, looked up, and said, "I don't think we will have to caucus in order for me to respond to your package. While you were in caucus, we developed several alternative plans, depending on the proposal put before us. I would like to..."

"Julian," Tony Cass interrupted, "may we caucus?"

"OK, Tony. Excuse us—we should not be gone long."

The association's team filed out into the hall and gathered around a watercooler. "What is it, Tony?" Julian asked.

"I think we ought to accept their offer," Tony replied. "I know that's not in one of our plans, but we are getting the extra pay for the extra hours and the raise is about what we expected."

"Why do you want to do that?" demanded Martin Good. "An hour ago we all agreed that, as a matter of principle, we had to have either the additional clothing allowance or the meal allowance added in our contract. You heard them—they are not going to allow a parity provision in the contract, so we are going to have to get parity one item at a time."

Julian looked to Don Blue for help. "What do you say?"

"I've been through this more times than I like to remember," replied the captain. "It's usually best to stick with a plan that you have had time to think about."

"Sorry, Tony," Julian said. "Let's go back in."

With all participants reassembled around the negotiating table, Julian began, "We would like to get this settled and have a tentative agreement that we can take back to our members as soon as possible—we hope today. We appreciate the withdrawal of your unit membership proposal. In selling that decision to your city council, it may help to use the cases we cited in our arguments. As you recall, those arbitration decisions and other rulings hold that lieutenants and captains may be a part of the fire fighters' negotiating unit if there is no evidence that this practice causes a subversion of supervision within the unit."

"Thank you, Julian," said Dean, "but I think we have those."

"If the city will offer a salary increase of 7 percent each year—that is, an additional 1 percent during the second year of the proposed contract—and if you will grant the clothing and meal allowances, I believe we have a contract," said Julian.

"I don't have to caucus to tell you that is not acceptable," responded Dean.

"Do you mean to let a 1 percent salary difference stand in the way of a settlement?" asked Julian.

"That is not all you're asking," responded Dean.

Julian cast a brief look at each of his team members, scribbled a note that he showed to Don Blue, received the response he wanted, and continued, "In the interest of getting a settlement today, we are prepared to make you a final offer. We withdraw our recent demand for an additional 1 percent increment the second year. If you will allow the clothing and meal allowances we request, we will accept all other conditions outlined in your proposal, including your latest increment proposal."

Dean exclaimed, "The fire fighters and the police get the same $400 clothing allowance. Knowing that we have not settled with the police unit, you're asking us to increase the fire fighters' clothing allowance by $100. If we do that, we might as well recognize that we must do the same for the police unit, too."

"Why is that?" asked Julian. "You won't accept a parity provision in the contract, yet you claim to be concerned about equity for the police unit. Why do you argue equity for them while denying it to us? The police have a meal allowance that you will not give to the fire fighters. Where is the equity?"

"We've gone over this. The police eat on the run while on duty; they do not go home."

"That's what you think," said Julian.

Dean ignored that remark and continued, "Fire fighters have a kitchen in the fire hall, where they can prepare their meals with the supplies they bring."

"That's the point: the fire fighters furnish their own supplies. That's why they want a meal allowance," Julian said.

"We are simply not going to adjust those allowances, given the other concessions we have made during these negotiations. I hope you will tentatively approve our offer and take it back to your members for ratification," said Dean.

"We will not take your offer, as it now stands, to our members because they will turn it down without one or the other of the allowances. Courts have held that a parity clause in a contract is not against public policy and therefore is enforceable in arbitration. Parity with the police unit is a high priority with our members. If your current position on that score is firm, we might as well call it a day. As far as we are concerned, we are at impasse.

You may want to consider how you are going to explain to a mediator that the police work a shorter week than the fire fighters do, get the same clothing allowance, receive a meal allowance that we don't have, and, on top of all of that, get ammunition and guns! The mediator will surely see the injustice here and recommend our proposal. If the mediator does not support our position, we are prepared to take the next step and submit to binding interest arbitration. We are confident we can win there." With that warning, the Professional Fire Fighters Association members filed out of the room.

Indeed, the meeting had ended.

HIS HONOR MEDIATES

"On that note, the fire fighters left, and I met you in the lobby as I was heading for my office," continued Dean. "I am sure they meant what they said—that they will not take our offer to their members. They will probably file a declaration of impasse, hoping to get support from the state-assigned mediator. And if they fail to get their way in mediation, they are prepared to present their case in binding interest arbitration."

"Will they get that support?" asked Mayor Hayes.

"Who knows?" Dean responded. "I think we have dealt fairly with them."

"The council guidelines allow a 14 percent salary increase over the two years, and you tell me that our last offer was 13 percent," said the mayor. "Would a seven-and-seven offer settle it?"

"I doubt it, but I really don't know because it was never offered. Jean would have opposed the idea. I didn't suggest it because we will need some flexibility during mediation, if it comes to that. This damn parity thing is the real bone of contention. The fire fighters want a raise in clothing allowance, and the Police Benevolent Association is holding to its well-publicized priority items: time-and-one-half compensation for overtime instead of straight time, and a substantial increase in meal allowance."

"Dean, suppose I tried to mediate this fire fighter thing?" asked Mayor Hayes. "I haven't been directly involved in the negotiations. As we're talking here, some ideas come to mind that might help clear this thing up."

"It may be worth trying, although you will have the council to deal with if you violate its guidelines," Dean warned.

Ed Hayes dialed Main Street Fire Station Number One. "Hello, this is Mayor Hayes. Is Lieutenant Martin there? May I speak with him? Julian, this is Ed Hayes. Dean Lee and I have been discussing this last negotiation meeting. I feel that it would be ill-advised to declare a formal impasse when we might settle this ourselves. I have some ideas I would like to present to both negotiating teams. Can you get your group together here tomorrow morning?"

"I believe so, if we can make some shift changes for the two fire fighters on our team," replied Julian. "Are you going to mediate this thing?"

"I want to help get a settlement. Have your team here by 10:00 A.M.—and thank you."

After hanging up the phone, the mayor turned to Dean and said, "Dean, I will meet both teams in the council room at 10:00 A.M. tomorrow. Wish me luck!"

"I will," replied Dean, as he prepared to leave. "I'd better find Jean and the chief."

At exactly 10:00 A.M., Mayor Ed Hayes entered the council chambers, took his place behind the ornate chair at the head of the polished table, and waited while the other people in the room found their usual places at the table. Still standing behind his chair, he said, "I want to express my appreciation to all of you for coming here today on such short notice. I hope that the result will be worth your effort. When I heard how your meeting ended yesterday, I suggested this meeting as another endeavor to arrive at an 'in-house' agreement on this contract. I ask you to consider the following proposals, which I hope will serve as a basis for discussion and a final settlement.

"First,..."

BUT, THE POLICEMEN GET GUNS!

Questions for Discussion

1. Why do you think the fire fighters changed negotiators when Don became captain?
2. Why do you think Chief McCarthy feels the way he does about bargaining?
3. Why do the fire fighters place such an emphasis on a parity provision in the contract?
4. How do you account for the lack of progress during the first six negotiation sessions?
5. What are some unique aspects of collective bargaining among police and fire fighters?

6. Why do you think the fire fighters are reluctant to merge with the police into one bargaining unit?
7. In the proposed trade-offs, are similar issues being traded?
8. If you were Mayor Hayes, how would you proceed to arbitrate this impasse?

PART FOUR

FROM IMPASSE TO SETTLEMENT AND THEREAFTER

The impasse stage in negotiation begins when one or both parties declare that further progress in reaching an agreement cannot be made without help. In most situations, either party, or both parties by agreement, may file a declaration of impasse. Public sector bargaining statutes in some states mandate that an impasse occurs automatically when agreement has not been reached by a specified date or deadline.

The inevitability of impasses impelled state legislators to incorporate impasse resolution procedures into statutes permitting or mandating public sector collective bargaining. The impasse resolution procedures involve third-party neutrals who use mediation or fact-finding strategies in an effort to help the parties reach agreement. Another impasse resolution procedure frequently mandated for police and fire fighters is binding interest arbitration, sometimes in the form of final-offer arbitration.

In a small publication entitled *Industrial and Labor Relations Terms: A Glossary*, Robert E. Doherty defines the following terms:

Mediation. An attempt by a third party, usually a government official, to bring together the parties to an industrial dispute. The mediator has no power to force a settlement. Although usually used interchangeably with "conciliation," mediation is sometimes distinguished from conciliation, conciliation being merely an attempt to bring the two sides together, mediation suggesting that compromise solutions are offered by the third party. (Doherty 1989, 22)

Factfinding. Investigation of a labor-management dispute by a board or panel, or by an individual, usually appointed by a chief executive of a government or state agency....Factfinding boards and factfinders issue reports that describe the issues in the dispute and frequently make recommendations for their solution....Several states have also enacted laws providing for factfinding to assist the parties in the resolution of labor disputes. (Doherty 1989, 13)

Interest Arbitration. Adjudication to resolve an impasse in contract negotiations. Infrequently used in the private sector, interest arbitration has, since the early 1970's, become widespread in the resolution of disputes in the public sector, particularly for police and fire fighters....(Doherty 1989, 19)

Final Offer Arbitration. A type of interest arbitration in which the arbitrator selects either the union's or the employer's final proposal. In some instances the arbitrator selects one side's entire "package," in other cases the final proposal of either party on each issue in dispute. Also known as "last best offer arbitration." (Doherty 1989, 14)

Mediation is customarily the first step in the conciliation process. A neutral third party works with the two parties at impasse—sometimes separately, sometimes together—in an effort to reach an agreement. The selection of the format for the discussions is usually the prerogative of the mediator.

At the initial meeting of the parties, the mediator attempts to help identify and confront the unsettled issues. In fact, the impasse may result from a dispute concerning the status of the issues. Which are settled? Issues may need to be reidentified or redefined. Most authorities recommend that the mediator confirm agreement on the issues to be addressed with a question such as, "When all of these issues have been settled, will we have a contract?" The response to this question is critical. If one or both parties respond negatively, the directory of outstanding issues must be addressed first. The parties must inevitably agree on a final list of unsettled issues. With that accomplished, the parties are ready for help in identifying alternative solutions to those problems.

The mediator attempts to learn what combinations of proposals and counterproposals have been discussed during bargaining. This information helps the mediator develop trade-off solutions that the parties may not have considered. These suggestions often require compromises that must be sold to both parties. Mediation works best in cases in which the parties have done their homework—that is, have prepared for mediation. The mediator's chances for success depend on the extent to which the parties trust the mediator and are willing to share confidences. The mediator needs to know whether there are hidden agendas.

Another problem that mediators sometimes face is mediating between factions on a negotiating team. Internal wrangling and disagreements within either the union's or the district's bargaining team make it very difficult to focus on the real issues. Sometimes the problems stem from the makeup of the team. Frequent points of disagreement deal with ranking the issues, packaging the issues, or deciding which issues are dispensable. Any hostility or infighting among the members, if it exists, must be addressed by the mediator before any attempt to deal with the contract issues is made. Case 16, "What to Do until the Fact Finder Comes," deals with these kinds of problems.

Some states impose statutory deadlines for the various stages of impasse resolution. For example, if agreement is not reached 100 days before the budget submission date, a mediator must be called in. If the mediation deadline expires without a settlement, a fact finder must be hired or appointed. This resolution process is very effective in settling impasses, especially when the final stage of fact-finding is binding. With statutory deadlines for impasse resolution, negotiating parties work more diligently for solutions during each stage of the process. Without enforceable deadlines, the parties frequently procrastinate and play the waiting game. Each party believes that a final settlement is more important to the other. In truth, it is equally important to each.

If mediation fails to achieve an agreement, the next step is fact-finding or interest arbitration, depending on what the statutes stipulate. Fact-finding is usually advisory—that is, nonbinding. Interest arbitration is binding arbitration. Occasionally, as in New York State, "essential" employees, such as police and fire fighters, are required to use binding interest arbitration, but all other public employees are allowed to work toward a final settlement through fact-finding.

The formal process of fact-finding is similar to that of interest arbitration. The fact finder presides at a scheduled hearing at which each party presents, with comments, a fact-finding brief citing its last position on the outstanding issues. Each party to the dispute is expected to provide written support for its position on unresolved issues. The testimony of qualified witnesses may be accepted also.

The fact finder, working as a neutral third party, assembles all the facts that were presented at the hearing, evaluates that evidence, investigates other facts if needed, and fashions recommendations in the form of a written report to the parties. The fact finder's report includes a discussion of the issues and recommendations for settlement that hopefully will be viewed as reasonable and sound. The fact finder usually presents a rationale and support for each recommendation.

Because the fact finder's recommendations are advisory and not binding, the parties have the option to accept or reject the report. If the fact finder's report is accepted by both parties, it forms the basis for a successor agreement. If the report is not accepted by one or both parties, the recommendations may serve as a basis for further discussion of the issues. Or the parties may completely disregard the recommendations and head back to the table to resolve their differences. In most states, the fact finder's report is provided to the media. It was thought that the parties would tend to temper unreasonable and outrageous demands if they knew that those demands would be brought to the attention of the public. Experience has shown that publicizing the report has not really served that purpose. Generally, the public has demonstrated little interest in fact-finding reports. What difference does it make, after the fact?

In the case of interest arbitration, the recommendations presented in the report are binding and thus provide a final agreement.

A major flaw in the public sector bargaining statutes of most states is the failure to charge the parties for impasse resolution procedures. In most instances, the cost of impasse resolution is borne by the state. Thus, the parties suffer insignificant financial pressure to settle before reaching impasse. With little more than time invested in the bargaining procedure, parties frequently play negotiation games, expecting that the conciliator will eventually solve their problems. States are not looking to revise their bargaining laws so that negotiating parties incur greater costs of impasse resolution procedures. Currently, approximately one-third of the states that use mediation in impasse resolution require the parties to share part of the costs. Of the states that use fact finding as an impasse resolution strategy, more than one-half require the parties to pay for the services of the fact finder.

TO STRIKE OR NOT TO STRIKE?

The federal government does not speak to the issue of public employees' right to strike. Thus, without federal laws and guidelines, the decision of whether to permit strikes by public employees is left to the states. The courts have consistently held that public employees have a constitutional right to be members of a union and, in most states, have the right to bargain collectively. The courts have also determined that the right to organize does not extend to the right to strike. The state legislature must grant that right. In the absence of legislative authorization, public employees do not have the right to strike. This decision is based on the common law rule of long-standing custom and past practice.

Of the more than forty states that allow some public employees to participate in determining salary and conditions of employment through collective bargaining, eleven states allow strikes. Ten of these states have legislated the right to strike: Alaska, Hawaii, Illinois, Minnesota, Montana, Ohio, Oregon, Pennsylvania, Vermont, and Wisconsin. The eleventh state—California—ignoring the common law doctrine, has allowed courts to authorize public employee strikes.

Every state that authorizes strikes by public employees excludes certain employees from the right to strike and mandates prerequisites that other public employees must meet in order to strike. For example, Montana has three public employee bargaining laws, each relating to a particular classification of employee. The rights and responsibilities of each classification are clearly spelled out. Pennsylvania has two laws: One law prohibits strikes by police and fire fighters, and the other stipulates strike conditions for all other public employees. In Alaska, public school employees are not considered "public employees" and are thereby excluded from using the authorized strike law for public employees. All states that allow strikes require public employees to attempt settlement through conciliation—usually mediation and fact-finding—before they exercise the right to strike.

States that authorize public employee strikes also mandate regulations and guidelines for the conduct of a strike. Among the constraints found in state laws are limits on the length of a strike, time periods within which notice of intent to strike must be submitted to the employer, ways the injunction may be used to prohibit or stop a strike, and policies for dealing with striking employees. Courts and state regulatory agencies have interpreted and clarified the regulations by issuing opinions and decisions on cases brought before them.

No public employer or employee group has provoked more court and agency decisions than have school districts and their employees. This has been in part caused by some of the unique features of the school district as an employer. For example, school districts have employed groups of people with many and varied "communities of interests." The typical school calendar has had a minimum of 180 days, which must be completed by a certain date. This calendar has imposed stress in prolonged teachers' strikes if management attempted to keep schools open and classes running by hiring substitutes, who may be paid more than the striking teachers. If the board refuses to allow the striking teachers back in the school, for whatever reason, the courts can and do declare this action a "lockout" and award teachers unemployment compensation for the days locked out. Case 18, "Fire the Teachers; Keep the Substitutes," illustrates the trauma, anger, and frustration that may result from a prolonged teachers' strike in a small community. When neighbor is pitted against neighbor, teacher against teacher, and parent against parent, the children are the victims caught in the middle.

Each of the eleven states that allow public employees the right to strike have placed restrictions on that right. Most states mandate that the parties try all impasse resolution procedures—mediation and fact-finding—before the employees become eligible to strike. Some states require that the current agreement expire and that an appropriate period of time elapse before a strike can occur. A strike can be prevented by a court injunction when there is reason to believe that the strike would pose a distinct danger to the health and welfare of the public. State courts have exercised wide latitudes in determining what conditions pose a threat. In his book *The Legal Structure of Collective Bargaining in Education*, Kenneth Ostrander lists twenty-two reasons that have been used to enjoin strikes as creating a clear and present danger. Some of these reasons are:

(1) It (the strike) would reduce per diem reimbursement to the school district if the 180-day school year is not completed by a given date.
(2) The expense for custodial and maintenance staffs would continue even if the schools were closed.
(3) The failure to complete the school term as scheduled might affect the school district's summer school program.
(4) The night school classes would be affected.
(5) The school could not be kept open.
(6) The P.T.A. would be disrupted.
(7) The parents' work schedules would be affected because their children would not be in school.
(8) The adult classes would be affected.

Ostrander comments on the courts' unpredictability and concludes that "any pretext becomes the basis for issuing an injunction." When issuing injunctions for any of the reasons cited above, for example, Pennsylvania judges made broad interpretations of what constitutes "a danger to the health and welfare of the public." (Ostrander 1987, 91–93)

When the right of public employees to bargain collectively was gaining momentum in the sixties, many authorities in the field, and others, believed that the state legislatures would hold the line on the right to strike. They were convinced that the public would not accept strikes by public employees and that most public employees would not choose to strike. Most of the states did hold the line. Reasons for denying the right to strike ranged from declaring public employees' services "essential" to the fear that the right to strike would give too much power to public employees at the expense of elected representatives of the people. However, what many observers failed to anticipate was that exclusive representation by unions would sometimes allow a minority of the members to make critical decisions for all employees. And that included rejection of proposed settlements and exercising the right to strike.

In states that did not allow the right to strike, the right to demonstrate and engage in picketing, which would not interfere with normal business operations, was usually accepted. On occasion, these seemingly unobjectionable actions got out of hand, unintentionally setting off a chain of events that contributed to a strike mentality. Legal demonstrations and picketing should be closely monitored and controlled so that they don't degenerate into histrionics and violence. Case 17, "Drifting into the Strike Zone," illustrates what might happen when (1) an exclusive representation policy permits a minority of employees to reject a fact finder's report, and

(2) employees and employers break off communication, and employees decide to demonstrate and picket but negligently allow themselves to blunder on toward a strike.

States that have not legislatively granted the right to strike do have strikes—but not as many. Research shows that the number of strikes is dramatically lower in states that exact a penalty for striking. New York's "two-for-one" penalty has proved to be an effective strike deterrent because it affects every striking employee. Public employees in New York do not want to suffer the penalty of loss of two days' pay for every day on strike. The penalty is not negotiable. The legislature mandates it, and that makes it effective.

CONTRACT ADMINISTRATION AND MANAGEMENT

With the advent of public sector collective bargaining, the middle manager in public organizations has taken on new dimensions and new roles. One of these is the major, critical role the middle manager plays in the administration of the negotiated contract. After the collective bargaining agreement has been signed by management and union representatives, the middle manager is the one who must administer the contract at the building or department level. The ultimate responsibility for seeing that the contract is administered uniformly and consistently throughout an organization rests with the chief executive officer. The importance of this management responsibility is cited in studies that show that, frequently, more management rights are given away through incompetent day-to-day administration of a contract than are surrendered at the negotiation table.

In order to administer the contract effectively and consistently, the middle manager must know all the contract provisions and how each is to be interpreted and managed. In addition, the middle manager must understand the roles of all other administrators in the organization regarding contract management. If middle managers have been a part of the ongoing contract negotiations, they probably have a fair understanding of the specifics of the contract and of the administrative roles. If they have been excluded from the negotiation process pertaining to employees under their supervision, the information that middle managers need to competently administer the contract must be provided in another way. Again, this is the responsibility of the chief executive officer.

Public and private organizations have found it helpful to conduct contract administration seminars for all supervisory personnel who may become involved in resolving questions about contract provisions. The chief executive officer might provide a draft document enumerating interpretations of potential problem contract provisions for group discussion. Although all aspects of troublesome provisions may be open for discussion, eventually one—and only one—interpretation of each provision survives. Thus, all managers have clear and identical guidelines for administering the contract.

Case 19, "But the Contract Doesn't Say That," illustrates what frequently happens when contract administration is not taken seriously.

SPECIAL COMMITTEES ADDRESS BARGAINING PROBLEMS

Public employers and employees are learning that matters of special interest to both parties but not dealt with in negotiation, for one reason or another, may be addressed in other ways. One means of addressing such matters is use of a joint study committee made up of representatives from both management and labor. Study committees have been used effectively to address issues that either were not accepted for negotiation or required research and intense study. The committee often deals with issues that are potential problems but are not worth holding up a settlement.

Although study committee recommendations may not automatically be translated into policy, both parties usually take them seriously. If study committee recommendations are not taken seriously, the issues in question tend to become priority issues for one party or the other in the next round of negotiations. Issues that study committees have successfully considered and resolved include teacher evaluation criteria and procedures, policies on attending conferences, changes in insurance carriers, curriculum matters, work schedules, safety issues, and problems involving civil service classification and job title.

Another kind of committee that is achieving great success, when organized and implemented correctly, is the labor-management committee (LMC). The LMC is usually described as a forum for discussion of and efforts to resolve matters of mutual concern. Basically, the LMC is a joint committee made up of union and management members who meet regularly to address the ongoing problems in the organization. Most authorities believe that the LMC has a better chance of succeeding when it is established and structured during good economic times. In other words, don't wait until a crisis develops before seriously considering what an LMC could do for your organization. It is also important that the parties involved are getting along and have a strong, amicable, professional relationship. The LMC is not an effective vehicle for pulling negotiation chestnuts out of the fire. Nor does an LMC take the place of normal contract negotiations.

Frequently, a neutral facilitator will be invited to discuss the purpose and organization of the LMC to help the parties get started. The facilitator's first job is to determine the degree of perceived need, or readiness, for an LMC on the part of the parties. The parties must demonstrate a willingness to share information and to embrace open communication networks. The parties must accept the concept of shared decision making. The facilitator looks for a commitment on the part of all members of the organization. When that commitment is confirmed, the parties are brought together to help design a committee structure.

In places where the LMC has been successfully organized and implemented, it has had a positive effect on the quality of the negotiation process. And it has reduced the number of grievances. Experience has shown that this kind of joint committee has had tremendous success in resolving many major disagreements without the need to file a grievance. The LMC's major advantage is that it is an ongoing process. Case 20, "Let's Try a Labor-Management Committee," deals with this successful medium—a promising trend in labor-management relations.

CASE SIXTEEN

WHAT TO DO UNTIL THE FACT FINDER COMES

Amy Oliver dialed the correct combination of letters the first time, opened Post Office Box AP, and pulled out the lone envelope. The return address in the upper left-hand corner indicated that it was the one she was expecting. She ambled over to one of the small counters in the post office lobby while opening the envelope. Leaning against the counter, she read:

September 20, 1993

Ms. Amy Oliver
Negotiator
Woolstock Education Association
P.O. Box AP
Woolstock, State

Re: Case No. 324-93

Dear Ms. Oliver:
    Enclosed you will find the appointment of a Mediator in the above-referenced case. The Mediator is :

Dave Brewster
Orange Grove, State

    The Mediator has been requested by this office to contact you directly to make arrangements for mediation.

May we remind you that the Mediator is limited in the number of days to be used for any individual case. Because of these limits, only issues of high priority should be brought to mediation.

Chief of Conciliation

cc: Dave Brewster

Although it was Saturday morning, Amy decided to drive by the high school to see if Dan Simon's car was there. As director of the school's computer center, Dan often opened the computer lab to students on Saturday mornings during the first few weeks of school. He believed in fostering the initial enthusiasm students had for the technology. Amy pulled in beside the familiar battered AMC Hornet in the parking lot.

Dan was helping a student at one of the many computers. When he noticed Amy, he motioned her to his office. After joining her there, he didn't need to ask about the letter she was already holding out to him. After reading it, he asked, "When can we expect to hear from this Dave Brewster?"

"Probably the first of the week—thanks to you," replied Amy. "He will also call Claudia to set up meeting dates."

"He will be lucky to even get meeting dates out of Claudia Richter," said Dan, smiling. "She negotiates as though salary raises come out of her pocket."

Amy was not smiling. She did not share Dan's perception of Claudia or his perspective of bargaining. In fact, about the only thing they had in common was the responsibility to negotiate a successor contract for the faculty. Amy said she would let him know when she heard from Brewster, and left.

THE CHANGING OF THE GUARD

By the end of his third year at Woolstock, Dan Simon had earned the reputation of being the district's most militant teacher. During that year, he campaigned for and won the presidency of the Woolstock Education Association (WEA). He beat Amy Oliver by two votes and was the first elementary teacher to hold that position. In the close election, Amy was reelected chief negotiator for the association, providing an unexpected and novel arrangement. The president of the association had always served as chief negotiator also. It had been that way since the teachers decided not to use hired professional negotiators.

During the election campaign, Dan criticized the senior secondary teachers' reign over the negotiation committee and its issues agenda. Few elementary and almost no young teachers had served on the committee. His campaign appealed to younger teachers by promoting flat-rate dollar raises rather than percentage increases, and a substantial increase in the pay for graduate hours and the master's degree. Dan won the support of the elementary teachers by promoting a fifty-minute daily preparation period for all teachers. Although all elementary teachers had at least two thirty-minute daily planning periods, none had a fifty-minute block of time, as the secondary teachers did. He publicly ridiculed a proposal by the high school faculty members of the negotiation committee that called for high school band and chorus directors to get the same extra curricular salary as the varsity coaches did. He pointed to this as indicative of what had been past practice in setting priorities for limited financial resources. More than a few teachers who had supported Dan's candidacy were now having second thoughts about his qualities of leadership and his professionalism.

THE MEDIATION DEBACLE

The initial mediation session was scheduled for Thursday at 7:30 P.M. in the high school boardroom. Dave Brewster arrived early in order to greet the participants as they arrived. This was not his first assignment in Woolstock, and he had been looking forward to working with Amy Oliver and Claudia Richter again. Claudia introduced Dave to Dr. Jeff Goodson, Superintendent of Schools, who was new to that position since the last impasse. The only other unfamiliar face was Dan Simon, who was introduced by Amy as the new president of the Woolstock Education Association. Dave remembered Linda Singer and Ron Palmer, teacher negotiation representatives, and Allen Barsky, the district board member.

With the four representatives of the WEA seated on one side of the large conference table and the three district team members on the other, Dave flipped the pages of a document he held. "The copy of the declaration of impasse you filed with the state, Claudia, indicates that the parties have held four negotiation sessions, during which six of eighteen original issues were resolved. Do both parties agree that the twelve issues listed in the declaration are the ones that remain unresolved?"

"We thought we had an understanding concerning the personal days issue, but I guess it was not written off," said Claudia. "So we assume those are correct."

Before Dave could continue, Dan Simon spoke. "I suggest that we try mediation with the parties in separate rooms. Obviously, we have not been very successful sitting across the table from each other."

Dave glanced at Amy to read her reaction to the suggestion, because she represented the WEA at the table. Amy looked up from the paper she had been studying. "Perhaps it would be best. We have had a few unfortunate incidents lately."

"Claudia, how do you feel about that?" asked Dave.

Claudia had taken a silent poll of the district's team and was ready. "We are willing to try almost anything that may lead to an agreement."

"Well, that's a start," said Dave. "Before we break up, I would appreciate having a copy of your recently expired contract and copies of the original association and district negotiation proposals. I'll need to refer to them as we move along."

"We will be in the teachers' lounge," said Amy as she picked up her materials to leave. "You remember where that is?"

"Sure do," replied Dave. "I'll meet with the district team first, if that's OK with you."

After the last member of the WEA team closed the boardroom door, Dave said, "What's going on, Claudia? This is the first time the parties in this school district have not worked through mediation together at the table."

"We have a new ball game," replied Claudia. "The difference is Dan Simon." She told him the story of the campaign and election and of Dan's anger when he was not named negotiator for the association even though he won the presidency. She described how Dan constantly interrupted negotiation proceedings and was forever demanding a caucus. Claudia continued, "Because of the way negotiations were being conducted, we had to change our tactics. Of the twelve issues still on the table, two are district proposals. We are holding those so we have something to negotiate. Of the six issues settled during our prolonged negotiation meetings, four were district issues. Two of our proposals were withdrawn, and the other two were agreed to in a mini-package compromise with the association."

"While I'm talking to the teachers, can you come up with something that I can use to start the negotiation process?" asked Dave.

"I'm not sure how hard we'll try," answered Claudia. "I doubt that our board will change its position on any of the issues unless there is substantial movement on the part of the association. That has been our problem right along. We have made significant moves in the past only to have the association take advantage of that and refuse any compromise on its part. I doubt we will do that again. It is their move. The ball is in their court."

Superintendent Goodson tapped his pipe on the glass ashtray to empty it, which also served to get the attention of the group. "We know the association is having internal personnel problems that have demoralized and hampered its negotiating committee. I personally believe that Dan Simon has no intention of settling short of fact-finding unless the district gives in on everything. The current position of the association on the unsettled issues reflects his campaign promises."

"It doesn't sound promising," Dave conceded. "See what you can do while I visit with the teachers."

As he left the boardroom, Dave could hear the loud, argumentative voices emanating from the faculty lounge and ricocheting off the walls of the empty hallways. When the teachers heard him coming, the voices stopped. Two unfamiliar teachers had joined the group. Dave learned later that they were elementary teachers who had dropped by when they saw the light on in the faculty lounge.

Dave wanted to start things off as pleasantly as possible. "Well, I asked the district committee to reconsider its last position on the outstanding issues. Now, what can you suggest that will help us get off dead center in these negotiations?"

"Before we discuss anything," said Amy, looking at the two visiting elementary teachers, "I think Al and Roger should leave."

"We're on our way," said Roger. "Good luck."

"You couldn't have helped hearing the argument we were having as you came in," said Amy. "Unfortunately that is all too indicative of the impasse we have right here within this committee. Dan and Ron want to maintain the hard line that the association has taken during these negotiations. Having been through this many times before, Linda and I know that we don't stand a chance of getting everything we are asking for. Linda and I have been trying to convince Dan that we must demonstrate a willingness to compromise on the remaining issues. I am at the point, personally, where either we get serious about honest negotiations and stop playing games, or I want out."

Dave Brewster looked at Dan and asked, "How do you feel about all of this?"

"For years, Amy, Linda, and other high school teachers who have been around a long time controlled the association and negotiated items that favored that group. Raises were always percentages, which gave the biggest raises to the highest-paid teachers. After that group had earned master's degrees and had taken all the graduate courses they wanted, compensation for graduate hours ceased to increase. The current contract mandates a fifty-minute preparation period for secondary teachers only.

"The younger faculty members and the elementary faculty now demand equity. That can begin with acceptance of the association's proposals for these negotiations."

"You're probably right," said Dave, "provided that the association is willing to negotiate its interests in the issues rather than just reaffirm its inflexible position on them."

"I have argued that we should reduce our salary demand if the district will agree to a dollar-amount raise rather than a percentage," said Amy. "We are not going to get $3,500 per teacher each year of the two-year contract. But the district might agree to the principle of an equivalent dollar raise for each teacher."

"Suppose we start with that and develop a mini package that I can take to management," said Dave. "What would be a more realistic equivalent dollar amount to ask for every teacher?"

Before Amy could answer, Dan interrupted, "Naturally,S we have a fallback position on the salary issue, but we are not prepared to reveal that now. If we do, the district will reduce it again in its counterproposal, and by the time we get to fact-finding..."

"Fact-finding!" Amy shouted at Dan. "Who in the hell is talking about fact-finding? Is that what this stalling has been about? You're expecting a fact finder to come in and settle this for you?"

Dan was visibly startled by this outburst. He avoided looking at Amy as he stammered, "If we don't come to an agreement in mediation, we will end up in a fact-finding hearing. I just don't think we should lay out our bottom line on the issues to the mediator."

Dave decided to try to cool things down. "My effectiveness as a mediator is related to the degree of confidence you have in me. If I am to help you develop new proposals, I need to know your priority issues and where compromises are possible."

"I think we should take a fifteen-minute break," said Amy. No one argued with that suggestion.

As Amy and Dave waited for their turn at the coffeemaker in the kitchenette, Amy suggested that they take a walk down the hall. Dave said that he would meet her after he checked with the management team to see what progress was being made there.

When Dave caught up with Amy in the hall, he smiled as he said, "Tough case. I haven't seen you that angry before, although I can't say I blame you."

"I'm trying to decide what to do," said Amy. "The association is not ready for fact-finding. I could not and would not try to defend all of the association's current positions in a fact-finding brief."

"Intentionally or not, Dan and his supporters have boxed themselves in," said Dave. "They committed the association to a lock-in tactic of bargaining. By promising extraordinary catch-up raises, more compensation for graduate hours and a master's degree, and a fifty-minute prep period for everyone, they won control of the association. Compounding the problem has been their consistent pledge to constituents that they will hold firm. They lose face and credibility if they back down now."

"And Dan naively believes that a fact finder will come riding in out of the west and pull his chestnuts out of the fire," said Amy.

"Probably," answered Dave.

"Well, we know that will not happen," said Amy. "So what do we do now?"

WHAT TO DO UNTIL THE FACT FINDER COMES

Questions for Discussion

1. Based on your experience, what problems and subjects of dispute surface during employee discussions and selection of appropriate issues for negotiation?

2. What do you see as the major problems troubling the Woolstock Education Association? Why?

3. What is your opinion of the way Dave Brewster handled the mediation session?

4. Why does Amy feel that the association could not defend its positions in fact-finding?

5. If you were the mediator, how would you answer Amy's last question, "So what do we do now?"

CASE SEVENTEEN

DRIFTING INTO THE STRIKE ZONE

It was unusually warm for mid-October—a bright and sunny Saturday afternoon with the temperature in the 70s. Les Cornell parked his car on the street a block from the school athletic field. That way, his car wouldn't be blocked in the school parking lot if he decided to leave early. Les hadn't been to a high school football game in years—probably not since his son Michael graduated. He hadn't planned to watch a football game today. When his wife Ann left the house to attend a neighbor's baby shower, he decided to take advantage of the weather and do something outdoors. He toyed with the notion of washing storm windows, but readily gave up that idea when he heard the high school marching band across town.

As Les walked the block toward the school driveway, he noticed small groups of people carrying placards and milling around the driveway entrance to the school and athletic field. His first thought was that it was a demonstration aimed at the large chain grocery store near the school entrance. Then he recognized the protestors to be local teachers from Cedar Point schools. Les assumed it was merely a publicity gimmick sponsored by a school organization—that is, until he could read the first poster carried high by one of the elementary teachers. It read, "Cedar Point Board Unfair to Teachers." The next sign proclaimed, "Teacher Power! Strike Now!"

Les couldn't believe what he was seeing. About fifty teachers, each carrying a sign, marched in an unending circle in the 100-yard-long driveway. When a car entered the driveway, the protestors moved to the side, allowing the car to pass, but kept the chain circling. Dumbfounded, standing in the grocery store parking lot alongside a dozen other citizens, Les was startled by a soft voice, "Hi Mr. Cornell, what do you think of this?" Becky Ryan had deserted the line of marchers and was heading in his direction carrying a sign at least as tall as her five feet, two inches. She was pointing to her placard, which read, "Teachers Deserve Fair Contract."

Les smiled. "I agree with the message. The method of delivery is something else." Les liked Becky Ryan. As one of the best elementary teachers in the Cedar Point school system, she is a model of professionalism. He knew that if Becky Ryan was pounding the bricks, or whatever the term was, there was trouble in Cedar Point. "What's going on?" asked Les.

"Hey, we're on strike," she said laughing. "See what you're missing by not being on the board? Now, don't you wish you had run for another term on the board?" Then she dropped the forced smile and the placard. "Actually, we're in a big mess. Last night the faculty negotiation committee voted to withhold all teacher supervision of extracurricular activities and athletics. We were called and asked not to work the football game today, and to picket the game and block the driveway. We're not blocking the driveway, but no teachers are working."

"I can hear the game from here," said Les. "Who is coaching?"

"Parents have taken over, and are they ever mad!" replied Becky.

"I am surprised to see you carrying that sign," said Les.

"I am, too," said Becky, smiling. "Grant Morton, the president of our association now, thinks that if we can convince the board that we mean business this way, we may not have to really strike. I hope he's right, because I would be against that."

"I can't believe it will come to that," said Les. It didn't come out as convincingly as he intended.

"I'd better get back to my protest," Becky said good-naturedly. "Enjoyed talking to you; say hello to Ann."

"Will do; nice talking to you, too," replied Les.

As Les walked up the drive toward the school grounds, he greeted the teachers carrying signs who looked his way. Many of them were hired during the ten years he served as president of the school board. And most of them had taught one or another of his children. The first staff member he saw not carrying a protest sign was the high school principal. Les asked where he might find Steve Kline, the school superintendent. The principal pointed to the school building. "The last time I saw him he was working in his office." As Les headed in that direction, he saw that the score was 32 to 10 in favor of the visiting team.

While walking toward the school, Les noticed that the breezeway between the junior-senior high school and the elementary building was now enclosed. That made sense, given the harsh winters. The Independent Cedar Point School District had consolidated with a half-dozen former rural school districts to form the Consolidated School District after World

War II. The K–12 enrollment of about 1,500, plus or minus 100, changed very little over the years.

When the state legislature allowed collective bargaining for all public employees, Cedar Point fared better than many school districts. Long before the concepts of school-based management and teacher empowerment became popular, the faculty and administration at Cedar Point demonstrated the many advantages of working together. Multiyear contracts were routine and usually signed before the budget voting date in June. Les wondered what had changed? Would Cedar Point teachers really strike?

Les found Steve Kline in his office, dictating into a mini recorder. Steve motioned him in as he finished a sentence and turned the recorder off. He came around from behind his desk, extending his arm to shake hands. "Les Cornell, it's really good to see you. You don't visit us often enough."

"Actually," said Les, grinning, "I came up to see the football game. When your teachers' special welcoming committee greeted me, I decided to find out what in the hell is going on. Thought I'd see you at the game instead of working on Saturday."

"As you can see, we have a problem," said Steve. "You know that Amber Hadley is president of the board now. Several board members are out of town, but Amber called an emergency meeting of the board members we could round up this morning to discuss the situation. The teachers' strike action was completely unexpected. They have said classes will meet Monday morning. Until further notice, teacher supervision of extracurricular services and activities has been suspended. But we are getting ready, just in case."

"You're anticipating a full-fledged strike?" asked Les incredulously.

"We don't know, but we want to be ready if it comes."

"Well, what are you doing to get an agreement? Shouldn't you be working toward that? Where are you in negotiation?"

Steve sighed. "You've probably read that we've been through mediation and fact-finding. Neither party accepted the fact finder's report. The negotiating teams met once to discuss the report, and that ended with the teachers walking out. At this point, I guess you could say we're in a period of suspended animation. No future meetings have been set."

"Does that mean," asked Les, "that you have given up, and both sides now prepare for the inevitable strike?"

"Of course not," said Steve, the irritation evident in his voice. "It's more like a cooling-off period. The school board will meet Monday night in a special meeting to discuss the situation. You are welcome to attend."

"I may take you up on that," said Les. "Tell me, what is it you were doing to prepare for a strike when I came in awhile ago?"

"Actually, I was dictating a letter to be sent out to all staff members, parents, and community leaders. In essence, the letter would clarify the strike issues from the board's perspective and tell how the district, in general, will handle the strike, if that happens. Mrs. Hadley and I thought we should have something prepared for the board meeting Monday."

"Will the board attempt to keep the schools open?" asked Les.

Steve reached for a legal pad on his desk. "I have been jotting down questions that the board should address, such as Should the schools be kept open? Are enough substitutes available? Will the nonteaching personnel stay on the job—maintenance workers, bus drivers?"

"Looks as though you've thought of about everything," said Les as he got up to leave. "I think I'll walk down and see how our team is doing with parent coaches. They weren't doing so well when I came in here. The teachers tell me parents are angry—very angry. I may see you Monday."

Les parked in his driveway and joined his wife on the back porch of their comfortable old colonial home. Ann had been waiting for him. Folding the afternoon paper with the picture and headline on the front page showing, she held it for him to see as he came up the steps. "Did you see this?"

"No, but I saw some of it firsthand and heard all about it," he answered as he scanned the article and picture. The picture was an eight-by-ten of the teachers picketing the football game, with Becky Ryan front and center. The headline read, "Teachers Strike! Refuse to Work!"

"The strike was the topic of conversation at the shower this afternoon," said Ann. "Sarah Pierce—you remember that nice home ec teacher—told us about the teachers' meeting last night. She is on the negotiating committee, you know. We couldn't believe what happened! During the discussion about whether to strike or not, Sarah and one other teacher spoke against the strike. Sarah said she didn't believe in teachers' striking and that most of the faculty felt the same way. Then she reminded her fellow teachers that a minority of teachers—only 41 percent—voted to reject the fact finder's report. Only dues-paying members of the union were allowed to vote, and obviously some didn't bother. That was not a mandate to strike, she argued. Some of her best friends were very upset with her. In fact, she claimed she was threatened in case she attempted to organize a group of teachers against the strike. Can a minority call the shots in a serious situation like this?"

"Sure, that's possible," answered Les. "This state has an exclusive representation law that allows one union or association to represent, in this case, all the teachers in bargaining. If the unit has a low paid membership, it is possible that less than 50 percent could support one cause or another. That's probably what happened here."

"Sarah said that some of her friends were quite angry when they learned she was coming to the shower instead of picketing the football game," said Ann. "Were there many picketing?"

"Over half the faculty," answered Les, "but that may not be indicative of the support for a real strike. Becky Ryan was marching, but her heart wasn't in it. She said she would not support withholding services from classes. Apparently the association hopes that this action will prompt the board to reconsider its position. Steve Kline is pretty certain the board will not back down. I wonder how Grant Morton is handling all of this. He has been a capable and honest association president for many years. I can't believe that he is very comfortable with all that is happening. I've always had a great deal of respect for him. I think I'll call him after dinner."

Grant Morton seemed pleased to hear from Les. He sounded tired and had good reason, with only two hours' sleep the night before. Les offered to call back the next day, but Grant seemed to want to talk now. He told Les about the many negotiation sessions, beginning in February, with far too many issues to settle. Glen Potter, the association negotiator from State Center, declared the parties at impasse in May. Two mediation sessions settled some of the issues, but, by then, each party had become entrenched in its position on key issues. Thus, the compromises proposed by the fact finder were allowed neither a fair hearing nor serious consideration.

"I hear that the teachers are equally divided on the issue of support for the association's position," said Les.

"There is no denying that," responded Grant. "The negotiating committee believed that a one-day demonstration during a major activity would convince the public that we had a cause and show the board we meant business. It appears to have backfired. The teachers' demonstrating today did not get much sympathy from the public, especially from parents. Some of us on the committee are concerned about the rift evolving in our ranks."

"And well you should be," said Les. "Sarah Pierce told Ann what happened at your meeting last night."

"That incident was unfortunate, and I have apologized to her. That's an example of why we have to settle this without any further confrontations."

"Would your committee be willing to reconsider the fact finder's recommendations?" asked Les.

"I can't speak for all the members but, yes, I think we would be more amenable to those suggestions than we were twenty-four hours ago," answered Grant.

"Last question," said Les. "If I can get the school board to go along, would you accept my services as an unpaid mediator in this case?"

"I would, and I'm sure the committee would go along," said Grant.

"I'll get back to you," said Les.

On Monday night, Les presented the same proposition to the school board. He would serve as an unpaid mediator if accepted by both parties. His only condition was that he would determine the format for the meetings. The board approved the plan, although several members voiced the opinion that not much would be accomplished unless the teachers backed down on most issues. Les was invited to meet with the teachers' negotiating committee, which also accepted his format condition.

The front page of the *Cedar Point Bell-Enterprise* carried the headline with story, "Former Board Member Mediates." An editorial in the same edition charged the parties to take their responsibilities seriously and work toward agreement.

THE AGREEMENT?

Les opened the meeting by reviewing the unsettled issues and the fact finder's recommendations on each. He said that he considered these recommendations fair compromises. But because the parties did not share his view, each should propose alternative terms for settlement. The board members continued to work in the boardroom, and the teachers moved to the library across the hall. During the next three hours, Les worked with the two groups, suggesting various options and alternatives.

The teachers accepted sharing health insurance costs, but only by those hired after the signing of the new contract. Demanding a contribution by current staff was a rollback and regression, they claimed. If the board approved that condition, the teachers would reduce their salary increase demand from 12 to 10 percent. The teachers had to have agency fee. The state and national organizations were pushing that. Too many teachers were on a free ride.

The board remained just as determined to not have agency fee in the new contract. The board offered to withdraw its merit pay proposal and to accept the fact finder's recommendation that a study committee address the issue during the next year, provided that the association drop agency fee. At this point, the board added a new chip—retroactivity. Should the economic issues be retroactive?

Les asked the teachers to join the board members in the boardroom. "I must confess that I misjudged the readiness of each of you to settle this impasse," he said. "I sincerely thought you wanted to avoid further confrontation. In three hours, we have raised only two potential compromises that might, in time, be approved. Even if that happened, each party is sitting on issues that it proclaims nonnegotiable. If we continue in that vein, how will we ever arrive at an agreement? I suggest we begin again, with very serious attention to the fact finder's recommendations.

"You will recall that you allowed me to set the format for these meetings. If we do not reach agreement tonight, I will consider scheduling a public hearing at which each party will be expected to explain its position on each recommendation made in the fact-finding report. I think the public would be interested to hear your rationale for refusing to come to terms with those recommendations. Now, I don't think such a meeting is necessary. I think we can settle this. I urge you to reconsider your positions on the unresolved issues. Consider whether your positions would stand up to a public airing. Don't allow the district to drift into a strike."

As the teachers left the room, one was heard to ask, "Can he really call a public meeting?"

Grant answered, "I don't know, and I don't want to find out."

DRIFTING INTO THE STRIKE ZONE

Questions for Discussion

1. How does a decision to strike affect the individual members of the union? What are some of the consequences?
2. What caused the Saturday strike demonstration in the Cedar Point school district?
3. Do you think Steve Kline was premature in his preparations for an all-out teachers' strike?
4. What are the advantages and disadvantages of exclusive representation laws?
5. What is your opinion of the way Les Cornell conducted the informal mediation?
6. What other issues are involved in this case?

CASE EIGHTEEN

FIRE THE TEACHERS; KEEP THE SUBSTITUTES

Jim Salwauk, 37-year-old superintendent of Valley Central School District, sighed again as he stared disbelievingly at the banner headline in the Saturday morning edition of the local newspaper, *The Daily Express*. The large black type read, "SUBSTITUTES SUPPORTED: PARENTS PROTEST TEACHERS' RETURN TO CLASSROOM," followed by a slightly smaller secondary head, "Public Meeting at 1:00 P.M. Today." Collapsing into his office chair, Jim scanned the article summarizing the conflict that had been smoldering in his school district for the past several months. After the teachers went out on strike a second time within a two-week period, parents demanded that the teachers be fired and substitutes be hired to complete the school year. Jim thought to himself, Nothing in my fifteen years of teaching or in my professional training prepared me for the confrontation I will face this afternoon.

It was 9:00 A.M. on a cold and sunless spring day. Jim tossed the newspaper aside, pulled several files from his desk drawer, and forced himself to concentrate on preparing for the 1:00 P.M. meeting. He found concentration difficult. Staring out the window, Jim frantically thought to himself, How did our school district get into this situation? What do I do now? Is it really my responsibility to get them out of this mess?

VALLEY CENTRAL SCHOOL DISTRICT

Located in a beautiful rural setting, Valley Central School District is the smallest of the eight school districts in Mills County. During the massive school reorganization movement in the early 1960s, Valley was the only county district that would not discuss merger with another high school district. Community citizens persuaded the school board to limit reorganization agreements to the non–high school districts that could send students to the local high school. Thus, the high school could retain its identity and remain a community school. Student enrollment, currently 625 in grades K–12, has steadily declined since 1975, but the number of teachers (forty-two) has remained approximately the same.

The economy of the area, particularly Mills county, depends primarily on agriculture and agribusiness. Diminishing farm income has resulted in hard times for many citizens in the community, and each year the number of boarded-up store fronts on main street increases. During the past four or five years, it has been increasingly difficult to pass school budgets. Two years ago, the voters approved the budget on the third vote only after it was cut drastically.

Two administrators besides the superintendent work in the district. The high school principal, in his first year at Valley, also serves as the district's guidance counselor. The elementary principal, now ending her twenty-seventh year, teaches music part time to elementary students. Valley Central School District used to serve as an unofficial training facility for new and inexperienced teachers. Teachers would take a position for a few years and then either quit the profession or move up and out to a larger school and better salary. During recent years, decreasing job opportunities swayed teachers to remain in the system, so that currently more than 60 percent have been at Valley for ten years or more.

THE PRINCIPAL CHARACTERS

James Salwauk is in his second year as superintendent at Valley. He has been a public school teacher and administrator for fifteen years: ten years as a high school teacher in another state and three years as high school principal in an adjoining school district. Acceptance of his current position was a way of breaking into the superintendency. His only negotiating experience was serving on the teachers' negotiating committee during his first year of teaching.

Roger Jones, president of the Valley board of education, is twenty-six years old and a lifelong resident of the community. He graduated from Valley High School eight years ago and was elected to the board of education four years ago. Roger has worked with his father in a farm implement business since dropping out of college during the first semester. He negotiates for the school district in the current contract negotiations.

Max Bennet is president of the local teachers' association and negotiator in the current contract dispute. He joined the faculty four years ago and teaches sixth grade. This is his first teaching position. Max is viewed as the most militant local association member and easily won the right to represent the association at the bargaining table.

Marilyn Toon is president of the local Parent-Teachers Association, a position she has held for more than ten years. Although not a school board member, she takes an active interest in school board business and is considered very influential in the community.

LEADING TO IMPASSE

The Valley Central School District (hereafter referred to as the district) and the Valley Teachers Association (hereafter referred to as the association) initiated the negotiation process for a new contract thirteen months ago, on March 5. At that meeting, to the surprise of almost everyone, Roger Jones announced that he would negotiate for the district. He rationalized that Superintendent Salwauk had been in office for only about a year, but he, Jones, had served on the negotiating team during previous bargaining sessions. Glancing at Mr. Salwauk, he continued, "However, the superintendent will be on the negotiating team and will serve as our advisor." Max Bennet said that he would again negotiate for the association.

The parties exchanged copies of bargaining proposals and agreed to begin negotiation in two weeks on March 19, the first regular scheduled negotiation date. Meetings were scheduled for the third Thursday of each month, unless amended by mutual consent or until a contract was signed.

Matters got off to a very bad start at the very first negotiation meeting: Max Bennet challenged the board president, "Before we begin the formal part of our negotiations, we would like some evidence that you are authorized by the board of education to negotiate for it."

Roger Jones was clearly shaken, "Authorized?"

"Yes," replied Max. "In the past, the superintendent or a hired person negotiated for the district. Did the board vote to appoint you district negotiator?"

"Of course, I represent the board and the district at this table," responded Roger angrily. "Do you think I would be here otherwise? I thought I explained at our first meeting why I was going to negotiate instead of Superintendent Salwauk. I want you to know I resent the question. Now let's get on with the issues."

Max replied, "I expect that your appointment as negotiator is stated somewhere in the board minutes of a recent meeting; we can check on that." He continued, "We reject outright your insulting offer of a three-year contract with a wage freeze. You people seem to be oblivious to the real world or what's going on around you. Must we continually remind you that we are the lowest-paid teachers in the county—in this whole area? And we again want to assure you that no school district, including Valley, is going to settle a three-year contract with a wage freeze. We can discuss some of the other issues, if you want, but there will be no settlement without a substantial salary increase."

"Well," said Roger, "we consider your request for a 10 percent salary increase each year of the three-year contract irresponsible. Most of you teachers live in this community, so you must know that, given present economic conditions, the public will not support a salary increase, much less a 30 percent raise over the three years. I suggest we adjourn until our next meeting date so you have time to reconsider your position."

Before Max could respond, Superintendent Salwauk interjected, "Could we have a caucus?"

Because neither negotiator objected, the board team left for the boardroom down the hall. After the door closed, Jim said, "I think *both* teams ought to reconsider positions, and I think we are ending this session way too soon without accomplishing anything. If we don't go back in there and have a positive discussion on at least some issues, what can we hope to begin with the next time we meet?"

"Well, what do you suggest?" replied Roger.

"I think we ought to go back and let them know that we are willing to negotiate on all issues, including salary, and at least tell them that both parties should reconsider positions for the next meeting. As I said before, I am uneasy about proposing a three-year salary freeze when we do intend to offer some increase. The freeze is a red flag."

Roger responded, "I don't think we should give false hope or play our cards this early. Besides, are you forgetting what the representative group from the PTA demanded at our last board meeting? The public in this community will not stand to have taxes raised, especially for teachers' salaries. And the school board is supposed to represent the public at these negotiations." The other board member on the team supported Roger. The first negotiation session ended, therefore, amid feelings of frustration.

On the morning of April 16, the date set for the second negotiation session, the association negotiator called the president of the board to suggest that the meeting be postponed or canceled. The reason given was that the information the teachers had requested from their state association had not arrived, and when it did, they would need time to put it together. After reminding Max that this was rather short notice, Roger said he would grant the request reluctantly. In fact, he was relieved to be free of this meeting because the district's position had not changed, and he had no idea where this was going.

The May negotiation meeting opened with the presentation of a revised salary proposal by the association. Max announced that, in light of information his group had received from the state association, including recent salary settlements in the area, the association was now proposing a three-year salary increase of 8 percent the first year, 9 percent the second year, and 10 percent the third year of the contract. This would average out at 9 percent each year of the three-year contract, and that was what most of the schools in the area were settling for. Max closed with, "If the district approves this salary proposal, the association is willing to reconsider a number of its other demands, including agency shop."

Roger Jones stared at each member of the association team and finally said, "I thought when you requested more time to collect additional information that you might realize the reality of the economic situation of this school district. We simply don't have the sources of funds that other districts you're comparing us with have.

Max asked, "Does that mean your position continues to be a salary freeze?"

"Not necessarily," Roger said. "We could offer a modest 3 percent increase each year, but it would come from funds saved by not replacing three teachers who will be leaving after this year and by eliminating some activity funds...."

Max interrupted, "That is outrageous and not at all acceptable to us!"

Roger slapped his papers together and stood up to leave. "Then I see no point in further discussion. I will inform the State Mediation Board that we are at impasse."

Over the summer, the state-appointed mediator made three attempts to settle the impasse, but to no end. The teachers returned to school in September under the terms of the previous contract. A state fact finder requested by the district held a hearing and, in November, issued a report with recommendations for settlement. The district rejected the report primarily because the recommendations included a salary increment of 7 percent for each year of the three-year contract. The association requested a meeting with the district during the first week of January and warned that, unless some significant progress was made, the teachers intended to go out on strike. On January 11, the teachers set up pickets and closed the school.

THE STRIKE

Thirty parents crowded the boardroom as the school board members gathered for the regular January meeting, three weeks into the teachers' strike. Roger Jones moved the group to the cafeteria so that all could be seated. Marilyn Toon, PTA president, received permission to address the board. "I have been asked to speak for this group, and I have some questions. What is happening in negotiations?"

Roger replied, "We met last week with the teachers and made very little progress."

Marilyn asked, "Is it true, as some members of our group heard, that the board is weakening in its resolve to hold the line on salaries?"

"That is not true, although we discuss that issue at every meeting."

"It is reassuring," Marilyn continued, "to know that our school board is representing the sentiments of most of the people in this community. We will not stand for any increase in taxes." Then, turning to the other side of the table, she addressed Superintendent Salwauk, "What are you going to do about classes? Is it possible to hire substitutes so we can run classes even if the teachers stay out?"

Jim replied, "We are hoping that this strike will be settled soon so we can get on with what we're supposed to be doing. I doubt that there are enough qualified substitutes in the area to staff the school, but the board has asked me to look into that possibility. Our sub pay of forty-five dollars a day is not very attractive."

"Well, we may just have to raise that," With that said, the parent group left the cafeteria.

Superintendent Salwauk scheduled the February 19 board meeting in the cafeteria, having been informed that a group of citizens would again attend. As the room began to fill, Jim noted that about half of the 100 or so in attendance were high school students.

Calling the group to order, Roger Jones announced, "I have asked Superintendent Salwauk to make an announcement."

Jim only glanced at his notes as he said, "At the direction of the board, I have hired substitute teachers who will begin teaching classes next Monday, when school will reopen. We regret that we have not been able to negotiate a contract agreeable to both parties, but that is the case. Buses will run at the normal times, and we hope to have all classes staffed within the week. I have also revised our school calendar, attempting to make up the days lost so far, and this, along with other information, will be sent to every household tomorrow morning. We ask for your patience and cooperation."

This announcement was greeted with cheering and applause by everyone except a few teachers, who left the room as unobtrusively as possible. The meeting ended with Marilyn Toon expressing the appreciation of the assembly to the board for its sensitivity to public sentiment and concern for taxes.

On Monday, twelve people were arrested when fights broke out between picketing teachers and the substitutes who were crossing the line. During the next two weeks, the presence of state troopers around the school kept order between the two groups except for the hooting and name-calling.

Two weeks after classes resumed, the teachers abandoned the picket line and notified the board of their intention to report for work. When the teachers tried to enter the school, parents and board members blocked their passage, turning them away with shouts of, "We want to keep the substitutes; they care about our children," and "Go find a job in the city where kids don't care."

At a hastily called meeting of the school board that evening, the teacher "lockout" was lifted when Superintendent Salwauk suggested that the teachers might be eligible for unemployment compensation if they were not allowed to return to work. The board members were surprised and more than a little perturbed to learn that the district's insurance company could, by state law, be held liable for the unemployment payments to the teachers.

When the teachers reported to school the next morning, they were greeted by a large contingency of parents protesting the school board decision allowing the teachers to return to the classrooms.

The two bargaining sessions held during the following weeks succeeded only in intensifying the differences and bitterness between the two parties. At the end of the second negotiation meeting, the teachers disclosed that a one-day strike would be called within two days to protest the board's unwillingness to bargain in good faith.

The district negotiator warned, "If you walk out again, substitute teachers will remain in the classrooms at least until a contract is signed. A group of parents is demanding that all striking teachers be fired and the subs be put under contract. Students tell their parents that the substitutes are better teachers and seem to care about them."

Two days later, the teachers formed picket lines for the one-day strike, and the substitutes took over the classrooms. When the teachers tried to return to their classrooms the next day, parents and school board members blocked the entrances. As the teachers left the school grounds, the group of irate parents turned on the nearest school board members. "How could you let it get this far?" one of them asked. Another demanded, "We want a meeting with the total school board as soon as possible; when can that be?" The board members looked to Roger Jones, who timidly replied, "I can try to schedule a meeting for Saturday afternoon at 1:00."

"We want to hear your long- and short-range plans for solving this problem, and those plans should include the firing of all striking teachers. After what they have done to this community, they don't deserve to keep their jobs!" shouted Marilyn Toon. "You board members have broken faith with this community."

When the crowd had dispersed, Roger headed for the superintendent's office. "Jim, this situation has gotten out of hand. Now the parents are blaming us for this mess. It's probably due to the bad press we are getting. The news media are having a field day. Have you seen those headlines and letters to the editor?"

"Of course, I have," replied Jim, "but what did you expect?"

Roger dropped into the nearest chair. "I don't know what to do next. Some parents want us to fire all the teachers and keep the substitutes. Others want us to get the teachers back in the classrooms like right now. Local merchants who are supporting the teachers complain that the antiteacher group boycotts their stores and tries to get others to do so. Now they want a town meeting on Saturday to hear our plan for ending this mess. Hell, we don't have a plan—you know that! We have been going from crisis to crisis. Can you come up with something by Saturday? If you can, I'll see that the board backs whatever you come up with."

Jim reached out and closed the folder that was conspicuously open on the center of his desk. As he placed the folder containing the draft of his letter of resignation in the middle drawer of his desk, he said, "You and the other members of the board have not paid much attention nor expressed much confidence in what I have had to say so far. You have preferred to listen to and appease the 'public,' whoever that may be. I happen to believe that this school district is worth saving, so I'll give it a try. Be here in my office with the other board members at 12:30 on Saturday. That will give me a half hour to outline my plan to you and the board before I lay it out to the lynch mob at 1:00.

THE PLAN

The knock on Jim's office door brought him back to the realization that it was "D day." He said, "Come in."

As the five board members filed in, each taking the first available chair, Jim thought, Will they really support me?

Finally, Roger spoke, "Well, we're here to hear and support your plan. What are we going to do?"

FIRE THE TEACHERS; KEEP THE SUBSTITUTES

Questions for Discussion

1. What is most significant about the principal characters in this case?
2. How well, in your judgment, did James Salwauk deal with the individual incidents in this case? How might he have handled things differently?
3. How do you think the teachers might have done things differently?
4. Why was the school board so easily swayed by public pressure as represented by Marilyn Toon?
5. How would you respond to Roger's final question, "What are we going to do?"
6. What other basic issues does this case pose for you?

BUT THE CONTRACT DOESN'T SAY THAT

David Brennan, superintendent of the Northbrook Central School District, settled back in his chair, put his feet up on his desk, and admired the budding flowers and trees in the concourse just outside his office window. May was his favorite month. It was usually warm enough to get in a round of golf before dinner two or three days a week. On weekends, he and his wife Margo worked to prepare their motor home for the anticipated traveling that the summer months allowed. He glanced at his desk calendar. In a little more than three weeks, the school year would end and his "downtime," as he called it, would begin.

Everything considered, it had been a good year. The State Education Department's evaluation of district programs had resulted in a few recommendations for improvement, but that was expected. As Superintendent Brennan explained, "Evaluators are expected to find some things wrong so that they have subjects for the recommendations they are expected to submit." But that was behind them now. The senior class students had earned an unusually large number of awards and scholarships. The right candidates had won the school board elections. The budget for next year was ready and should be approved by the voters. The new high school principal seemed to be working out even though he was a little too gung ho at times.

The superintendent's speculation on what metal woods might do for his golf game was interrupted by his secretary, who tapped on his door and walked in with the mail. "It looks like the usual. You may want to answer the letter on the top of the pile before you go home. The university wants to know whether you plan to finish that study you started two years ago. We could probably get to it after commencement."

Brennan smiled and shook his head. "I don't know; we'll see. I do have other plans for this summer."

The superintendent was sorting out the circulars and advertisements to be discarded when the intercom signaled an incoming telephone call. It was his secretary. "Mr. Adams is on the other line and is asking to talk to you right away. Are you available?"

"Put him through." Brennan was not anxious to talk to Cecil Adams, the district business manager, simply because Cec's calls usually meant a problem.

"Hello, Dave," said Adams. "I just had a call from Jim Baker that you should know about, if you don't already. Jim said that if we didn't pay him for the personal day he took last week he would file a grievance."

Brennan paled at the word *grievance*. "What personal day? Why wouldn't we pay if he took one? Do you know what in the hell he is talking about?"

"That's what I was about to tell you. It seems that Jim Baker applied for a personal day, which was granted by the high school principal, Mike Thompson. Yesterday, Thompson found out that Baker used the personal day to substitute for a friend in the Loganville high school. He was paid regular substitute wages for the day. Thompson called him in this morning and gave him hell. He told Baker he was going to notify me to withhold payment for the personal day. I haven't received that memo yet, but I expect that it is coming. And Baker says that if we don't pay, he will file the grievance."

"Damn!" said Brennan. "It would have to happen to the president of our teachers' association. I don't want a grievance. We haven't had one in the fifteen years I've been here, and we're not going to start now. Let me know when you get the directive from Mike Thompson," he said as he slammed down the phone. He snapped on the intercom to his secretary's office. "Mrs. Rate, get me the high school principal at once. Tell him to drop whatever he is doing and get over here, now!"

TRANQUILITY IN NORTHBROOK

David Brennan accepted the superintendency of the Northbrook Central School District fifteen years ago. He came to Northbrook from a smaller school district in the central part of the state, where he had served as superintendent for six years. At the time, he had offers from other districts—some from out of state. His investigation revealed that the superintendents who left Northbrook inevitably moved on to administrative positions in much larger and better-paying school districts. He intended to use Northbrook as a stepping stone in his long-range plan for the superintendency of a large city district from which he would retire.

Sometime between his fifth and tenth years in Northbrook, Brennan's long-range plan was forgotten and he settled in. After the first few years, he took over as chief negotiator for the district. The school board did not take much interest in negotiation, considering it a nuisance that they had to tolerate. As long as things ran smoothly, the board was perfectly willing to let the superintendent run the show.

Brennan took great pride in the fact that no employee had formally filed a grievance during his tenure as superintendent. Several years ago, a union-appointed negotiator for the nonteaching union persuaded a custodian to file a grievance. When the custodian came to pick up the grievance form, Superintendent Brennan asked to speak to him. The grievance form was never completed and filed. That year, the nonteaching union successfully negotiated several proposals that had been priority issues for years.

Superintendent Brennan viewed himself as a model democratic administrator who practiced school-based management. He seldom met with his five building principals as a group. Periodically, he proudly proclaimed that he hired the best principals that he could find and that the district could afford, and then let them run their schools. Thus, Northbrook became a training camp and stopover place for middle managers. Last year, the high school principal resigned, after three years, to accept the superintendency of a small school district in the county. Michael Thompson came to Northbrook.

Three communities in the southwestern corner of the county merged to form the Northbrook Central School District as part of the state push for consolidation during the early fifties. The population of the three communities totals about 6,000, with Northbrook's 3,500 the largest. The district supports one senior high school, one junior high school, and two elementary schools in Northbrook, and one elementary school in each of the two smaller communities. The economy of the area depends chiefly on agriculture and agribusiness. A new shopping mall on the edge of Northbook and the usual main street stores in each of the communities serve the dwindling population of about half the county.

THE END OF TRANQUILITY

Mike Thompson knocked on the door and entered the superintendent's office. "What's up?" he asked innocently.

"What the hell do you mean, 'what's up'?" said Brennan, motioning him to close the door and then waving a document he was holding. "I have just been rereading the personal leave section of the teachers' contract. Have you read it?"

"So that's what this is all about," replied Thompson. "Yes, I've read it. Why?"

"Jim Baker called Cecil and said that he would file a grievance if he wasn't paid for the personal day last week. Did you know that?"

"I didn't know he called the business manager, but he told me the same thing when I said that I would stop payment for the personal day," said Thompson. "Do you know that he substituted in another district that day and got paid for it?"

"Yes, Cecil told me. Jim was wrong to do that, but as I study our contract language, I'm not sure he violated the contract."

"Of course, he did," said Thompson, raising his voice. "We can't have teachers taking personal days to teach in other schools so they can draw two salaries. Not only is it immoral and unprofessional, it is cheating our kids. I had to hire a sub to take his classes that day. That's wrong."

"I didn't say it wasn't wrong. I said that, given our contract language, I doubt we can win the grievance. Listen to this language, 'Four (4) days will be allowed per year for personal business. All such requests shall be made to the principal on a printed form, signed by the teacher, containing the following language: "It is understood that personal days shall not be used to extend any holiday or other vacation. It is also understood that the concept of a personal day only covers activities the teacher cannot do just as readily on his or her own time." Except in cases of genuine emergency, all requests for personal days shall be submitted for approval at least 24 hours in advance of the day or days involved.' Now what part of that was violated?" asked Brennan. "Did he give 24 hours' notice? Did he..."

Thompson interrupted the interrogation, "Yes, he gave me 24 hours' notice. But he deceived me. Jim did not tell me that he was going to teach in another school that day. Teaching in another school is not personal business. I admit my mistake was in not asking him directly and specifically why he needed the personal day. I usually don't ask because I want the teachers to know that I trust them. I guess in this case that was a mistake. When I talked to him yesterday, he admitted that he did not tell me what he was really going to do because I would have denied the personal day. And I would have. Dave, he cannot get away with this. If he does, we might just as well stop asking for reasons for personal days."

"What would you say if I approved paying him for the day?" asked Brennan. "That way you need not back down and there need not be a grievance."

"I would say that you undermined the authority of your so-called administrative team. I want you to know that I am not going to back down on this. Jim will not be paid unless you overrule me and authorize payment. If he files a grievance, it will get to you because I will not reconsider my decision. You should also know that this problem is known throughout the school. Jim is betting that we will back down. If you override my decision, the school board and others in the community will surely question why you think their taxes should subsidize such an extravagant absurdity."

"And if we lose in arbitration?" asked Brennan.

"The contract language will have to be addressed during the next round of negotiations," answered Thompson. "I will appreciate your support."

"Maybe Baker won't file a grievance after all. If he does, I'll let you know my decision," said the unhappy and disheartened superintendent.

The business manager deducted a day's pay from the next paycheck James Baker received. Baker filed a grievance, which, not unexpectedly, was supported by the Northbrook Teachers Association. Michael Thompson did not reconsider his decision, which was supported by Superintendent David Brennan and finally by the board of education. The final step in the grievance procedure was binding arbitration. Everyone, including Jim Baker and the association, was surprised by the arbitrator's ruling. In essence, the arbitrator ruled that, because the situation did not run afoul of restrictions cited in the contract, the district was directed to pay the grievant for the personal day.

Superintendent David Brennan was livid. As he feared, at the next board meeting it was suggested that the school's attorney review the language in the current negotiated contracts to ascertain weaknesses or flaws that should be addressed during the next round of negotiations. The board president suggested that it would be prudent to have all future contracts reviewed by the attorney before board approval.

Several days after the arbitration hearing, Lisa Jo Sullivan, principal of one of the Northbrook elementary schools, called Thompson. She said that she and Doug Bishop, principal of the other Northbrook elementary school, would like to meet with him. Would he be free tomorrow afternoon? It was the middle of July, two weeks before the principals' summer vacation would start. Mike Thompson said that he would welcome the opportunity to interrupt his scheduling conflict project. He liked Lisa Jo and Doug and looked forward to the meeting the next day.

When they were settled in the casual chairs around Mike's office with their soda and coffee, Lisa Jo turned serious. "We—that is, the other principals—watched the recent grievance situation with a great deal of interest. It was the first grievance in this district that any of us can remember. It's too bad we had to lose it, but it was worth it."

"Yes," Doug broke in, "every principal in this district has had comparable contract violations, or at least misunderstandings, but couldn't do anything about them. Brennan simply would not entertain the thought of a grievance. He considered a grievance a challenge to his integrity as the chief school officer and district negotiator. We've had our first grievance, which we lost, and the world didn't end. Maybe now things will loosen up around here."

"Don't bet on that," said Mike. "I have a feeling Brennan will never forgive me for pushing him into that one."

"Maybe not," said Lisa Jo, "but now is the time to again bring up the subject of contract administration. We tried before. We should be able to convince him now that if all administrators in the district agree on how our labor contracts will be interpreted and administered, we stand a good chance of avoiding grievances. We should be able to convince him that the next grievance will probably be won by the association on a past practice charge, because each administrator is left to interpret the contract language in his or her own way. At a meeting to discuss contract administration, we could also identify contract language changes that should be made."

"You are right, of course," said Mike, "but I'm not the one who should approach him about the meeting. We haven't said a word to each other since the arbitration hearing."

"Why don't we present the idea to him in the form of a petition signed by all five principals?" suggested Lisa Jo. "He can hardly ignore the fact that we see this as a common problem that needs attention. If we do it now, he will have time to think about it before school starts in September."

"I like the idea of a request signed by all the principals," said Doug. "However, I doubt that Brennan will give it much attention before September. Mike, will you help draw up the petition or whatever it is we're calling it?"

"Sure, provided that we can do it before August. After that, I disappear with my family to our cabin at Lake Okoboji."

THE GRIEVANCE

The new school year began without a hitch the day after Labor Day. Teachers returned to school for three days of orientation and in-service workshops before the first day of classes. A deeply tanned and amiable Superintendent Brennan addressed the assembly of teachers on opening day. He welcomed the teachers back; introduced the new teachers, extending them a special welcome; and expressed the hope for another banner year. He then introduced the five building principals, who would assume responsibility for the building meetings and workshops.

On the first day of classes, each of the building principals received a letter from the superintendent thanking them for the suggestions in their "summer memorandum." He said he would give the recommendations serious consideration.

On Monday of Thanksgiving week, Dan Cole, a high school science teacher, asked for an appointment with the principal sometime after 2:15 P.M. during his free period. When Dan entered the principal's office, Mike came around from behind his desk to greet him. Mike didn't know Dan

Cole very well. Dan was a loner who seldom mixed with the teachers in the faculty lounge. After small talk about looking forward to the coming three days off for Thanksgiving, Mike asked, "Dan, what can I do for you?"

"I have a rather unusual request," said Dan. "I have an opportunity for a part-time job at the radio station here in town, but the problem is they want me to start at 2:30. I have a free period every day beginning at 2:15, so it wouldn't affect my classes."

"You have a planning period every day from 2:15 to dismissal at 3:00," corrected Thompson, "and teachers are on duty until 3:30. I have a real problem with this request and I'm inclined to deny it."

Dan opened up his notebook and pulled out a copy of the teachers' contract. He flipped it to a marked page and said, "The contract doesn't prohibit teachers from leaving early; it just says that permission must be given by the principal."

Thompson asked to see the contract. "But it also says that the hours of regular service for classroom teachers will be 8:00 A.M. to 3:30 P.M. in grades K–12," he said.

"Meg Wendry over at the elementary school leaves at 3:00 almost every day because she has a baby-sitter problem," said Dan. "She has permission to leave early at least four days a week. Another teacher I heard about at the junior high gets out early every Thursday for some reason."

Thompson's impatience was beginning to show. "There is nothing I can do about teachers in other buildings. I'm sure they are not leaving before student dismissal. You are asking to leave at 2:30 and..."

Dan interrupted, "If you can't see 2:30, could I get out at 3:00?"

"If we're negotiating this now, I'll propose regular dismissal time at 3:30," said Thompson.

"You may not know that several years ago I was permitted to work at the station when they needed a substitute or extra help. It wasn't steady, but I left school early maybe two or three times a month—with permission, of course."

"No, I didn't know that," said Thompson, rising out of his chair. "In any event, I have another appointment in a few minutes. Why don't you stop by tomorrow about this same time, and I'll let you know my decision. In the meantime, I would like to have you think about why the contract stipulates specific service hours for teachers."

"Sounds to me as though you have already made up your mind," said Dan as he walked out.

On Tuesday morning, before he had a chance to take off his coat, Mike Thompson's secretary informed him that Superintendent Brennan wanted to see him immediately. Mike smiled as he hung up his coat and said, as he closed the door to his office, "Please get the superintendent on the phone." When his intercom signaled a call, he picked up the phone, "Mike Thompson here."

"Did you get the message that I wanted to see you?" asked Brennan.

"Yes, just a few minutes ago when I came in. I have a meeting with our PTA officers in half an hour, which should go most of the morning. Can we make it later this afternoon?"

"What are you going to do about Dan Cole? He asked if he could see me during the lunch hour today. Are we going to have another grievance?"

"Well, when I see Dan Cole at 2:30 today, I'm going to tell him that..."

BUT, THE CONTRACT DOESN'T SAY THAT

Questions for Discussion

1. What does Superintendent Brennan's response to his secretary's question about the overdue university study tell you about him?
2. Do you agree with Mike Thompson's decision to withhold personal leave pay from James Baker because he substituted in another school for pay? Why or why not?
3. Do you agree with Superintendent Brennan's view of himself as a model democratic administrator? Why or why not?
4. What do you think are the reasons for Superintendent Brennan's almost paranoid fear of grievances?
5. Was the petition by the principals the appropriate measure to force the superintendent to address a long-overdue issue? Why or why not?
6. How would you answer Dan Cole's request to leave early? Why?
7. What other issues does this case raise for you?

LET'S TRY A LABOR-MANAGEMENT COMMITTEE

The word was out. Even before the morning coffee break, most of the support staff had heard that all-night marathon negotiations had again ended in failure. The Oak Grove City School District and its Service Workers Union were no closer to a successor agreement. Time was running out. The tension and frustration in some way touched the lives of almost all the nonteaching employees in the district.

At 3:30 P.M., Susan Todd, school attorney and chief negotiator, entered School Superintendent Ken Glaser's office and was greeted by his secretary, Betty. "Go right in; he's expecting you," she said, smiling.

"I'll bet he is. Did he leave here at all?" asked Todd.

"He went home for a couple of hours this morning, but was back before noon," answered Betty. "He had a luncheon meeting with contractors, and they just left."

Dr. Kenneth Glaser, a tall, wiry, deeply tanned man in his early fifties, was standing staring out the window and watching children play on the elementary school playground across the street. "Wouldn't it be great to be over there playing touch football?" he said without turning around.

"If I had a choice," said Todd, "I'd rather be signing off on a new agreement with our service employees. I've come to resent the reproachful look I'm getting from employees around here when I come on campus. I don't remember that happening before, and I've been negotiating here for over a dozen years. Tell me it's my imagination."

"I'm afraid I can't," said Glaser. "You and I are the messengers—the bearers of bad tidings." Ken moved across the room to take one of the chairs around the small conference table in the far corner of his office. He motioned Susan to join him there and continued, "We are the ones who tell them that the school district will offer no more than a 4 percent raise. They know that the teachers settled a two-year contract with an 8 percent salary increase each year. They also suspect that the district administrators will receive about the same percentage. The union negotiator, Gary Garber, repeatedly reminds us that all the other school districts in the county that have settled with nonteachers are paying at least 6 to 8 percent increases. And our board is not about to double the number of union leave days from five to ten, as they requested. Most of our board members feel that the additional leave days would be used to conduct more grievance hearings. Then, to rub salt in the wound, we want our service workers to now pay 20 percent of the cost of their health insurance package. It's no wonder they're demoralized and grumbling."

"I thought for a minute there last night that the board might take your suggestion to raise its salary offer to 6 percent and to drop its health insurance proposal if the union would withdraw its demand for additional leave. That might have settled it," said Todd.

"It might have, but it didn't fly."

"Where do we go from here?" asked Todd. "The only solid agreement to come out of our twelve-hour marathon last night is the decision to meet one more time before giving up and declaring impasse. The agreement we have on the other four substantive issues is tentative, pending a final settlement of the salary, health insurance, and union leave issues."

"There may be some room for movement on health insurance," replied Glaser. "Salary is another matter. What support we had was lost when the city street and sanitation workers agreed to a contract with a 4 percent salary increase. Our board wants to use that as the standard. Four or five of our board members feel that the two unions are comparable and should be paid the same. You heard one of our board members—I think Dan Packard—say that we would have no trouble replacing any of our service workers if they quit tomorrow. So why give them a higher raise than the city gave its workers?"

"Yes, and the abrasive behavior of the union's negotiating team at the table, particularly their negotiator, Garber, has not helped proceedings. He turns board members off. Board members have claimed that their local businesses have suffered because of prolonged and adversarial negotiations. Last night, LaVon Norman again brought up her pet peeve—the increasing number of grievances in this district over the past few years. Other board members also look upon our number of grievances as a form of harassment. When is your next school board meeting?" asked Todd.

Glancing at the wall calendar, Glaser answered, "Actually, a week from tonight. Can we get a labor- management committee proposal ready by then?"

Susan stared at Ken in disbelief and then began to smile. "I don't believe what I'm hearing. I've been trying to get you to propose an LMC to the board for months. Why now? Do you think this is the time to propose another issue?"

"I don't know," answered Glaser. "Your arguments for a labor-management forum have not been lost on me. I wish now that I had bought your reasoning that the committee should have been established and structured during good economic times—when things were going well. Is this an appropriate time to propose it?"

"In my opinion, any time is a good time, as long as it works and both parties realize what they are getting into," said Todd. "What do you have in mind?"

"Actually, I'm grasping at straws. Suppose we were able to convince the board that there is a way to head off and perhaps eliminate grievances and at the same time improve personal relationships."

"Careful," said Todd, "you cannot guarantee that a labor-management committee will eliminate grievances. An effective committee would certainly reduce grievances and build a better working relationship between management and labor. When it works, it improves morale."

"Exactly," said Glaser. "As hometown people, our service workers have a high degree of credibility and many friends in the community. Board members are sensitive to criticism by these employees. Confrontational negotiations and our grievances have not improved our school-community relations.

I think the board members would buy into the labor-management committee concept if they were convinced it would end all this bickering. The question is, would the union go for it?"

"I'd say yes," replied Todd. "Garber has a successful teachers' committee in progress in another district. By and large, the unions have been supportive of committees. I think the unions see the LMC as a step in the direction of teacher empowerment and site-based management. However, Garber will expect something in return because this will come across as a district proposal."

"How will this scenario play?" asked Glaser. "Both parties agree to the concept of a labor-management committee—contract language to be worked out with a consultant from the State Conciliation Office. The union withdraws its demand to double the number of union business leave days in exchange for the district's withdrawal of its health insurance proposal. That leaves salary as the only outstanding issue."

"If the union is convinced that the committee will give employees more decision-making power, I'm sure they'll buy it—if the salary is right. The union's rationale for doubling the business leave days all but disappears. Employees will not have to dip into their personal days for griev-ance hearings if there are few, or no, grievances. But that does leave salary."

"I say we go with it," said Glaser. "What do we have to lose? I think I can convince the board to offer a 6 percent increase, and that might bring closure. Sue, you start on the proposal for the school board, and I will work on Dan Packard and LaVon Norman. Both of them have been concerned about grievances, so they just might be interested in the proposal. If we have their support, we stand a much better chance."

Susan Todd's presentation to the school board was very thorough and convincing. After a question-and-answer session, LaVon Norman asked Superintendent Glaser for his recommendation. Glaser strongly supported the concept of the labor-management committee, highlighting some of the advantages mentioned in Todd's presentation. He suggested that the board offer a package proposal to the service workers that would include a 6 percent salary increase and the organization of and guidelines for a labor-management committee, with all other issues to be dropped.

Susan Todd explained that if the board and union approved the plan, a representative from the State Office of Conciliation would meet with the parties to explain the whole process and procedure. Board member Dan Packard unexpectedly lent his support to the proposal, saying, "Relations between management and this union are characterized by such high levels of distrust and personal animosity, it can't get much worse."

The Oak Grove Service Workers Union used the better part of a two-hour caucus to debate the merits of the district's proposal. As pre-dicted by Susan Todd, Gary Garber supported the forum proposal. How-ever, the union demanded that the district drop its health insurance proposal and not have it as a first agenda item for the committee. After a long caucus by the district's team, this last condition for a successor contract was met. Both parties agreed that the specifics of the labor-man-agement committee would be discussed after the meeting with the state-appointed facilitator.

THE INFORMATION MEETING

Frank Bowen, representative of the State Office of Conciliation, opened the meeting with a story. The story was about a supervisor in a machine shop. The supervisor maintained power and status over his group of workers by carefully shielding the work assignments and production quotas for the day on a clipboard that he kept close to his chest. He doled out information on a need-to-know basis, bit by bit. The result was mismatched parts, ruined products, and much waste. A time-manage-ment expert was brought in to solve the problem and improve production. The solution was simple: he took away the supervisor's clipboard and posted the assignments and quotas. Conditions improved when information was shared by all the workers through the posting of assignments and quotas on a bulletin board visible to all. When the workers shared responsibility for quality control and production quotas, the problem evaporated.

"I am here," Bowen continued, "to tell you about a relatively new concept in labor-management relations. The labor-management committee works when the parties honestly want to share responsibility for improving the quality of education. If you have questions as we go along, feel free to ask them. I understand that you have a tentative agreement on a new contract that awaits language pertaining to a labor-management forum, if you agree to organize one.

"What is a labor-management committee? It can be described as a voluntary committee formed by the interested parties and made up of representatives of management and labor. The purpose of the committee is to identify and work for resolution of problems of mutual concern. Another important aspect of the LMC is that it provides a nonadversarial forum for ongoing dialogue and discussion. The labor-management committee meets on a regular basis."

Board member Norman raised her hand. "How does the labor-management committee relate to the negotiation process?"

"Good question," said Bowen. "It is important that this forum not be considered a substitute for collective bargaining. Nor does it replace the grievance procedure. When it works, the committee influences bargaining style and is a useful adjunct to the bargaining process because it deemphasizes adversarial relationships. When it works, the forum reduces the number of grievances. It provides an opportunity to discuss areas of disagreement and hopefully resolves them without formal charges being filed.

"Now, how do you get started? Obviously, one way is to ask the conciliation office to send someone to provide information and answer questions. Here I am. The office regularly schedules workshops around the state to provide information about its services. Sometimes those meetings serve as information distribution centers.

"When the decision is made to organize a committee, you request a facilitator to help get the process started. The facilitator's first job is to determine the degree of perceived need—of readiness for the process. The facilitator is looking for a commitment on the part of the members of the organization. In a joint meeting with the parties, such as this, we address questions such as 'How do you feel about this?' 'What do you understand about this process?' 'Will time be available for meeting during the workday?' 'What do you want this process to accomplish for you?'

"The facilitator will probably ask permission to meet with each team—management and union—separately. Speaking confidentially, the facilitator may again ask some of the questions mentioned before and perhaps others, such as, 'What's going on here?'

"After the caucuses, the facilitator will again convene the joint committee to appraise it of common concerns—common denominators. Then the facilitator will help design the structure of the committee."

"I was just going to ask how many serve on the committee?" said Glaser.

"There is no recommended number," replied Bowen. "A typical committee has four to six representatives from management and the same number from the union...."

"Who chairs the committee?" asked Dan Packard.

"That will be decided as we structure the committee. A common arrangement for a group like yours is to have co-chairpeople. In this case, it could be a member of the administration and a member of the union."

"What is your role after we get organized and going?" asked Dan Packard. "Do we solo?"

"Oh yes, you do!" replied Bowen. "However, your facilitator will continue monitoring to see how things are going and probably will attend several of the first meetings as an observer."

"I have one last question," said Dr. Glaser. "Is it unusual for a school district like Oak Grove with three separate unions to have a labor-management committee with only one of those unions?"

"It is not unusual," said Bowen. "In fact, that is exactly the way most LMCs get started. Our experience has been that labor-management committees are contagious. One successful committee will often spur interest by other units to establish their own committees. So, if your venture is successful, you may soon have two more committees in the district."

Because there were no further questions, Dr. Glaser and Mr. Cain, president of the local union, thanked Mr. Bowen for taking the time to attend the meeting and to explain the committee system.

When Frank Bowen had left the room, Superintendent Glaser stood and said, "I suggest we take a break to stretch and then reconvene to discuss the committee idea."

Gary Garber interrupted, "Although I'm in favor of a stretch break, I can tell you right now the employees are in favor of the concept of a labor-management committee. Why don't we take the time to caucus and have each party come back to the table with a last best offer. I think we should wrap this up tonight."

"We would be willing to try that," said Susan Todd. "I suggest we concentrate on salary. If we can agree on that, perhaps the other few issues will fall into place."

LET'S TRY A LABOR-MANAGEMENT COMMITTEE

Questions for Discussion

1. What major issues are involved in this case?
2. Do you agree with Susan Todd's premise that labor-management committees should be established during good economic times? Why or why not?
3. How does the labor-management committee relate to the regular negotiation process?
4. How did the settlement of a contract between the city and its street and sanitation workers affect the school district's negotiations?
5. Why do nonteaching school personnel generally have a higher degree of credibility with the community than any of the other school employees?
6. What do you see as the advantages and disadvantages of a labor-management committee?
7. Discuss the importance of the readiness of the parties in the organization and implementation of a labor-management committee.

Bibliography

ASHBAUGH, CARL R., KASTEN, KATHERINE L. KASTEN. 1991. *Educational Leadership: Case Studies for Reflective Practice*. New York: Longman.

BACHARACH, SAMUEL B.; AND EDWARD J. LAWLER. 1981. *Bargaining*. San Francisco: Josey-bass Publishers.

CARNEGIE FORUM ON EDUCATION AND THE ECONOMY TASK FORCE ON TEACHING AS A PROFESSION. 1986. *A Nation Prepared: Teachers for the 21st Century*. New York: Carnegie Forum on Education and The Economy.

DOHERTY, ROBERT E., ED. 1979. *Public Access: Citizens and Collective Bargaining in the Public Schools*. Ithaca: New York State School of Industrial and Labor Relations, Cornell University.

DOHERTY, ROBERT E., *Industrial and Labor Relations Terms: A Glossary*. Fifth Edition, Revised. Ithaca: Ilr Press, Cornell University.

EDUCATIONAL POLICIES COMMISSION. 1964. *The Public Interest in How Teachers Organize* Washington, D.C.: National Education Association and American Association of School Administrators.

LEFKOWITZ, JEROME, ED. 1985. *The Evolving Process—Collective Negotiations in Public Employment*. Fort Washington, Pa: Labor Relations Press.

NATIONAL COMMISSION ON EXCELLENCE IN EDUCATION. 1983. *A Nation at Risk: The Imperative for Educational Reform*. Washington, D.C.: U.S. Government Printing Office.

NATIONAL EDUCATION ASSOCIATION. 1965. *Guidelines for Professional Negotiation*. Washington, D.C.: National Education Association.

OSTRANDER, KENNETH H., 1987. *The Legal Structure of Collective Bargaining in Education*. New York: Greenwood Press.

Webster's Ninth New Collegiate Dictionary, S.V. "parity."